Michael Beck's to-hell-and-back conversion, ...
be the church even better than some of the highest moments of Christian
literature. Just as Jesus founded his church at the gates of hell, a church which
isn't hell-bent for heaven doesn't deserve the title "church."

> **—Leonard Sweet**, best-selling author, professor, and founder of The Salish
> Sea Press, SpiritVenture Ministries, and PreachTheStory.com

Michael Beck's new book will break your heart in the best possible way. His
deeply personal stories of humanity's brokenness will tempt you to close its
pages and shut your eyes to the pain. But if you do, you will miss the most
remarkable story of God's redemptive power to turn the ashes of depravity
and desperation into a stunning masterpiece of healing and hope.

> **—Missy Buchanan**, popular speaker and author

'Your God will restore everything you lost; He'll have compassion on you;
He'll come back and pick up the pieces from all the places where you were
scattered' (Deut. 3:1-3).   Michael Beck has written a personal testimony that
will encourage the hurting and wounded to trust God who redeems and
restores the broken.

> **—Lonnie Earnest**, Christian 12 Step Ministry, Inc.

I often mention Michael Beck when I refer to Jesus asking, 'who do you say that
I am?' Michael responded to this question with, 'He was my cellmate!' That
made an indelible mark on me. Michael found the One who could change
his life around and he wants the world to know this One who can do the same
for us. Generational trauma is real and he has experienced that and so much
more. If you are afraid of reading a raw and real book about life, stay away from
this one. But, if you want to experience the transformational power of Holy
Spirit and the God who can heal any and every generational curse or trauma,
then, by all means, dive right in. Thank you Michael for inspiring us.

> **—Rev. Dr. Dee Stokes**, lover of Jesus, author, leader, speaker

Spirituality is reality. God takes us as we are and works to make us people who
live in the new creation. Michael Beck's story is a powerful testimony to the
reality of God's transforming grace, and it is a reminder that the same grace is
offered to us as well.

> **—Dr. Steve Harper**, Director of the Wesleyan Studies Program at
> Northwind Theological Seminary

There is power in the practice of authentic testimony to a God who brings life out of death. This is Michael Beck's story, and he places his journey within the larger narratives of scripture, spiritual wisdom and recovery. God has never ceased to transform and heal us. Michael Beck bears witness to what all of this can mean. I needed to hear his story, again. I hope you will come to know it too!

—**Bishop Ken Carter**, Florida and Western North Carolina Conferences, The United Methodist Church

This book made me love and admire Michael Beck even more. *Painting With Ashes* is a wonderfully honest and deeply insightful story of radical conversion set in the frames of the tragic human narrative as this intersects with God's prevenient grace in Jesus. The result is a genuinely poignant, intelligent, and meaningful, witness. Captivating!

—**Alan Hirsch**, award winning author of numerous books on missional theology, spirituality, and leadership, founder of Movement Leaders Collective

Confessional, raw, and honest are the best words to describe Michael Beck's *Painting With Ashes* as he describes how the curveballs, mess-ups, and missed opportunities in life do not have to be the final word in one's story. They can become the starting point for healing and wholeness. Beck's journey will break your heart, make you reflect on your own life and encounters, and fill you with the dangerous hope that all things are possible.

—**Rev. Dr. Roz Picardo**, church planter, professor, and author, Mosaic Church and United Theological Seminary in Dayton, Ohio

This was like reading a Henri Nouwen book – if Henri Nouwen was an alcoholic with a drug addiction and had a criminal record, that is. Despite a background of substance abuse and violence, Michael Beck has found the deep kind of healing Nouwen wrote about. In this comforting and inspiring book, Michael invites us to see how Jesus can make all things new, not by wiping away our past completely, but by reworking what we've been through and leading us in the direction of true human flourishing. This is beautiful work.

—**Michael Frost**, Morling College, Sydney, Australia

Michael Beck's book is wonderful. I was riveted to every page, deeply moved, exhilarated and spiritually revitalised.

—**Michael Moynagh**, author of *Church for Every Context* and *Church in Life.*

Painting With Ashes is a must read for Christians at any level in their journey. Now in my 50th year of ministry I was reminded of how God has used and will continue to use my own weaknesses to display divine power. Michael Beck uses powerful examples to demonstrate the fact that our greatest asset is in fact our greatest brokenness.

—**Mike Slaughter**, Founder & Chief Strategist, Passionate Churches, LLC

Painting With Ashes is more than just the powerfully raw, ruthlessly honest and relentlessly hopeful story of God's work in Michael's life. It also offers deeply rooted, spiritually alive, and powerfully practical guidance for any faithful person who knows that God always has more for our lives that they have already experienced. By seeing what God is up to in Michael's life, every reader will be challenged to discover more of what God is doing in their own.

—**The Rev. Dr. James A. Harnish** is a retired United Methodist pastor and the author of *A Disciple's Path* and *Finding Your Bearings: How the Words that Guided Jesus through Crises Can Guide Us*

What a great read this is! With the pace of a novel and the dexterity of a surgeon, Michael Beck weaves his own story with those of many others to make clear God's desire and ability to transform lives. Testimony and teaching combine to produce a positive, persuasive and so-much-needed message to each reader - that ultimately God wastes nothing and none of us are beyond the touch of divine, re-creative, purposeful love. Even those who don't believe it! Read it. Then buy copies for those who come to mind, who also need to paint with ashes.

—**The Rev. Dr. Martyn Atkins**, former Chair of Fresh Expressions UK, General Secretary of the Methodist Church in Britain and Superintendent of Methodist Central Hall, Westminster

A can't-put-down, gut-wrenching story that I couldn't recommend more, Michael Beck's *Painting with Ashes* shows how God brings beauty out of the most desperate places. By weaving his story together with that of others who rose from difficult circumstances, Beck proves that each one of us is qualified to become a wounded healer. Beck also exposes what not just we, but also the church can be at our best. It is a necessary book for anyone looking to find their place in God's story and teach others to do the same.

—**Oneya Fennell Okuwobi**, Teaching Pastor 21st Century Church

Painting with Ashes is a powerfully-written life story that's both heart-rending and awe-inspiring, filled to overflowing with both brokenness and redemptive healing through God's miraculous grace. Stories from scripture woven throughout come to life with illuminating, soul-convicting relevance. Especially, the compelling instructive picture of all God's Church is intended to be provides an urgent call to leaders everywhere.

—**Rev. Sue Nilson Kibbey**, Director, Bishop Bruce Ough Innovation Center, United Theological Seminary, Dayton, Ohio

Michael Beck is a prolific writer and influential thought leader in innovative forms of ministry in North America. In this book we are introduced to the raw, unedited life story behind the movement maker. We see Beck's journey shift from a hurt person hurting others to a healed person healing others—a shift that begins with a Bible slid through his jail cell door. Beck takes us on a profoundly difficult journey through the depths of pain and addiction to the heights of loving community found in AA and the local church. Ultimately, Beck reminds us that in Christ our greatest asset is our brokenness and a masterpiece can be painted with ashes.

—**Luke Edwards**, Associate Director of Church Development for the Western North Carolina Conference of the United Methodist Church

Painting With Ashes reads very much like a fiction thriller, except for one thing...it is no fiction. You hold in your hands a powerful description of God's redemption in the life of a man with first-hand experience of the healing power of Jesus Christ.

—**Joseph Okello**, Professor of Philosophy and Ethics, Asbury Theological Seminary Dunnam Campus

PAINTING
WITH
ASHES

MICHAEL ADAM BECK

PAINTING WITH ASHES

When Your Weakness Becomes Your Superpower

Plano, Texas

PAINTING WITH ASHES
Copyright 2021 by Michael Adam Beck

All rights reserved.

No part of this work may be reproduced or transmitted in any form or by any means, electronic or mechanical, including photocopying and recording, or by any information storage or retrieval system, except as may be expressly permitted by the 1976 Copyright Act or in writing from the publisher. Requests for permission can be addressed to Permissions, Invite Press, P.O. Box 260917, Plano, TX 75026.

This book is printed on acid-free, elemental chlorine-free paper.

Hardcover: 978-1-953495-12-9; Paperback: 978-1-953495-13-6; eBook: 978-1-953495-14-3

All scripture quotations unless noted otherwise are taken from THE HOLY BIBLE, NEW INTERNATIONAL VERSION®, NIV® Copyright © 1973, 1978, 1984, 2011 by Biblica, Inc.™ Used by permission of Zondervan. All rights reserved worldwide.

Scripture quotations marked BSB are taken from The Berean Bible (www.Berean.Bible) Berean Study Bible (BSB) © 2016, 2020 by Bible Hub and Berean.Bible. Used by Permission. All rights Reserved.

Scripture quotations marked KJV are taken from the Holy Bible, King James Version (public domain).

Scripture quotations marked NRSV are taken from the New Revised Standard Version of the Bible, copyright 1989, Division of Christian Education of the National Council of the Churches of Christ in the United States of America. Used by permission. All rights reserved.

21 22 23 24 25 26 27 28 29 – 10 9 8 7 6 5 4 3 2 1

MANUFACTURED in the UNITED STATES of AMERICA

To the great cloud of *witnesses* who loved me into being.

CONTENTS

Nobody escapes being wounded. We are all wounded people, whether physically, emotionally, mentally, or spiritually.
The main question is not, "How can we hide our wounds?"
so we don't have to be embarrassed, but "How can we
put our woundedness in the service of others?" When our
wounds cease to be a source of shame, and become a
source of healing, we have become wounded healers.

Henri Nouwen, *The Wounded Healer*

FOREWORD

"Hey, Dad. You want to go with me to a recovery meeting tonight?" Nathan asked.

"Sure, son. Where?" I responded.

"At your church, stupid," he said with a laugh.

I picked Nathan up at his halfway house and drove into the church where I had been the lead pastor for more than twenty years. But I had never driven into the church like this in my two decades. I was there for him, my sweet boy, who for more than a dozen years had struggled with drug addiction and the accompanying, all-too-familiar arrests, jail time, recovery programs, homelessness, suicide attempts, and relapses.

This drive into Grace Church's parking lot was different.

We arrived at 7:30 p.m. as the Bible study that had been meeting in the Connections Café let out. A beautiful stream of mostly fifty- to seventy-year-old Grace Church people, dutifully carrying their Bibles, filed out the double doors of our church lobby. I sat in the car with Nathan and watched as another crowd of about twenty-five young adults, mostly in their midtwenties, smoked cigarettes in our designated smoking area. We didn't enter the church through the lobby but through the side door of the café because it's closer to the smoking area. (Yes, our church has a smoking area.)

When we sat down, I was clearly the oldest guy in the room. There was one guy in his forties, I'd guess, and the rest were Nathan's age. The Narcotics Anonymous meeting that had met at the church I pastor was convening. Sadly, other than walking by and giving a polite pastoral wave, I had never sat in the room with this remarkable group of recovering addicts. In the next hour, I heard the f-bomb dropped at least seventy-five times, but laced into the conversations were honest, genuine words of hope and healing coupled with sad words of failure and regret.

As Nathan and I left, I thought about the Bible study that had met the hour before in that very room. The participants were working verse by verse through the book of Philippians. They love Jesus and the church. The meeting room was a holy place, filled with holy people, doing holy work. Yet, in the next hour, twenty-five millennials had gathered. They never mentioned Jesus. The Bible was never brought out. The participants' language was raw. Yet, their meeting, too, was a holy place, filled with holy people, doing holy work. I could feel the presence of God.

You've heard it said or you've said it yourself: "You can't say that in church." We usually use the statement to chastise some poor soul whom we see as rough around the edges. Somehow, we have come to believe there are certain behaviors, words, and experiences that we need to leave in the church parking lot. I think this is bad theology and practice. When we falsely think that church is only for "holy," we imagine that we can leave all the unholy stuff outside. But then we are less whole and healed. Church needs to make space for the raw, ugly parts of life too.

As you read *Painting with Ashes* by my dear friend Michael Beck, you'll be tempted to think or even say out loud, "You can't say that in church." Michael's story is hard. It's raw. It's real. It's honest. He sometimes drops the f-bomb. But keep reading. Keep listening, because as he tells his story as it has been lived on the rough streets of Ocala, you'll hear the whisper of the Holy One. I teased Michael that we needed to put the recording industries label "Parental Advisory: Explicit Content" on the cover. Michael's story is explicit. Yet, woven through this amazing story is biblical depth and social commentary on things like justice, racism, addiction, education, and mental illness.

This is not just one man's story. It is our collective story. It is a story of healing and redemption that just might change your life.

Jorge Acevedo, Lead Pastor
Grace Church
May, 2021

A PARABLE:
CHILDREN IN THE ASHES

. . . to bestow on them a crown of beauty instead of ashes.
Isaiah 61:3

The remnant smolders in an ashy ruin where a home once stood. Pinpoints of heat glow beneath the surface. Smoke wafts free in the wind, billowing into the sky.

In the middle of the seething heap sits a group of children, their bodies smeared with ashes. They are an ordinary group by most standards, but they convene together in the desolation. One has big, almond-shaped brown eyes, dark hair, and an outdated bowl cut. He's sitting in the middle of the wake of whatever this disaster was. His head hangs limp, shoulders shrugged. A gentle rain sets in, releasing dark spires of ashy smoke. As the embers are quenched, the smoke clears.

Suddenly, the little boy and his companions spring to life. As they play in the ashy mud, a massive canvas appears. The brown-eyed boy smears the canvas with muddy ash, creating picturesque scenes with smudges and wipes.

He's painting with ashes. Canvas after canvas appears, and the others, a whole community of children of every conceivable color and shape, begin painting together. A society of artists. Children of the ashes.

As they play and dance and laugh and paint, seedlings spring up from the ashes. In the weeks to come, flowers, bushes, fragile little trees will grow from the ruins, until what was once an ashy heap, a barren landscape, the waste of yesterday's dreams, has become a garden of life. These children are creating a new world as they paint with their ashes.

In some way, all God's children are given their own smoldering heap to play in. We each have a fiery house of yesterday. We all have wounds that will never fully heal. But we have also been given the rain and a blank canvas, so that we can paint with ashes too.

I've been learning, thinking, speaking, and writing about God most of my adult life. I've attempted to shepherd people all across the spiritual map into deeper relationships with a God of their understanding. A brief study of the great women and men who have thought about God across the religious spectrum shows that many can't satisfactorily answer questions regarding the consistent presence of suffering and evil across the ages. And yet God sends prophets to tell us boldly that there is beauty in the exile and ruin of ashes.

One such a prophet, by the name of Isaiah, stood in the smoldering ashes of his society and saw beauty. Amid the people of his tribe, ambling around in the dust of what once was, he heard a word from the Lord . . .

. . . *to bestow on them a crown of beauty instead of ashes.*

It takes faith, imagination, and good old-fashioned guts to proclaim such a message of hope in the ruins of exile and destruction. Perhaps we are in such a time again.

Society as we once knew it has been laid to waste, its demise accelerated by a global pandemic. A globalized, hyper-connected network society is emerging. We live in the exile lands between what was and what's coming soon. We sit in the ashes of post-Christendom, post-truth, and post-progress.

We are one of the most stressed-out generations in history. Extended exposure to mental or physical duress ultimately becomes trauma. We are living through a series of unfolding crises that are causing individual and collective trauma on a massive scale. These overlapping crises include not only COVID variants, but systemic racism, inequality, poverty, climate change, political extremism, corrupt justice systems, an overdose epidemic, and the disintegration of church as we know it… just to name a few!

Unresolved trauma spills out in patterns of harm and can be passed on generationally.

Why do people feel Christianity does not offer an authentic and meaningful spiritual path? Why is "spiritual but not religious," usually aimed negatively at the Christian church? Why do so many Christians feel as if something is missing? If Jesus offers us healing, forgiveness, and a life of peace, why do so many Christians struggle with guilt, shame, and unforgiveness? Why does so many people's experience of church seem to fall short of actually dealing with the brokenness they try to hide? Or worse, why do so many report having been wounded by the church itself?

For many, the church is perceived as a place of harm rather than healing.

How do we help each other share our own stories, come to terms with our woundedness, and find healing with others? In a world fascinated with authenticity, how can we help each other share openly about our deepest struggles rather than concealing them?

The purpose of this book is to help you, the reader, experience a deeper level of healing. Simultaneously, it's my hope as the writer to experience healing as well. I'm not writing as some expert removed from the subject matter, but as someone on the journey alongside you, learning how to paint with my own ashes.

Contrary to the lives we digitize, filter for Instagram worthiness, and viralize across our social media screens, everyone is healing from something. There is no such thing as a person who is not on a journey of healing. We are all in a sense "in recovery" from some wound, mistake, or brokenness.

I used to think that if I could just be righteous enough I could please God. Now I realize it's not my righteousness that delights God, but my brokenness. It's the cracks that let the light in. I can't be good enough, long enough, hard enough to make God love me. God already loves me, just as I am, not as I should be. It's more a matter of grace than of effort, of receiving rather than giving. When I yield my brokenness to God, God uses it in incredible ways to bring healing to others.

I've discovered firsthand the truth of Jesus' words spoken to one biblical author, the apostle Paul: "My grace is sufficient for you, for my power is made perfect in weakness" (2 Cor 12:9).

If Christ's power is made perfect in our weaknesses, then our wounds become our superpowers.

If God can bring beauty from ashes, then ashes are the best materials we have to paint with.

On May 27, 2019, Greta Thunberg was on the cover of *Time* magazine as one of the "Next Generation Leaders." The *Guardian* described her global impact as the "Greta effect." Among her many accolades and awards are being the youngest *Time* "Person of the Year" and inclusion in the *Forbes* list of "The World's 100 Most Powerful Women" (2019).[1]

Her activism using social media and digital platforms against climate change has engaged millions of young people around the world and has brought global awareness to the issue. She has impacted the world in a profound way, all before she turned eighteen.

In earlier years, Greta suffered from depression and was diagnosed with Asperger syndrome, a mild form of autism. Leading up to the diagnosis, when she was just eight years old, she became depressed after learning about a lack of any serious response to climate change. At age eleven, she stopped talking and eating and lost twenty-two pounds in two months. Once Thunberg was able to convince her parents to change their lifestyles and reduce their carbon footprint, she found hope and the courage to believe that she could make a difference.

Greta famously refers to her medical condition as a "superpower."[2] She has transformed her challenge into an opportunity, what some would consider a weakness into a strength. She is painting with ashes on a global scale.

One of the primary spiritual mentors from whose work I draw is Dutch Catholic priest, professor, writer, and theologian Henri J. Nouwen (1932–1996). Nouwen believed that to be wounded is to be blessed. It is a gift.

Henri taught at the University of Notre Dame, Yale Divinity School, and Harvard Divinity School, as well as other academic institutions. At age fifty-four, after decades of teaching and enjoying the prestige of an upwardly mobile life, Nouwen took a journey of "downward mobility" to live and work among people with intellectual and developmental disabilities at the L'Arche Daybreak community in Richmond Hill, Ontario.[3]

Nouwen shared about his homosexual orientation openly with friends and alluded to it in his private journals. Yet he never announced this lifelong personal struggle publicly. He seemed unable to reconcile his priestly vows of chastity with a desire for physical and emotional intimacy. And yet, through his talks and prolific writings, Nouwen embodied a spirituality of compassionate vulnerability that brought healing to millions of people across the globe.

Nouwen believed this "spirituality of vulnerability" was exemplified most fully by Jesus in the incarnation. In Christian theology, the word *incarnation* refers to God the Son being embodied in human flesh in Jesus of Nazareth. This is God up close and personal, not a distant God above us or far removed, but one who can be touched, embraced, and even wounded by our hands. Jesus risks entering fully into our human condition—the beauty, the joy, and the pain. He lives out for us what it means to be human, embodying how to love God, neighbor, and ourselves.

In the New Testament there is a letter, named Philippians, that was authored by the apostle Paul during one of his imprisonments. In the second chapter, Paul inserts a poem that most likely predates him. It is a creedal statement, probably sung as a hymn, that preserves the church's earliest beliefs about Jesus:

> Let the same mind be in you that was in Christ Jesus,
>   who, though he was in the form of God,
>   did not regard equality with God
>   as something to be exploited,
>   but emptied himself,
>   taking the form of a slave,
>   being born in human likeness.
> And being found in human form,

he humbled himself
and became obedient to the point of death—
even death on a cross. (Phil 2:5–8 NRSV)

A humble posture of this nature inverts the dominating lust for power and prestige that typifies the Western world. This countercultural spirituality exemplified in the person of Jesus will be my guide for this book. In the self-emptying of Christ (kenosis) we see a God of downward mobility, who enters fully into the human experience in a total posture of vulnerability . . . a baby in a manger, a subjugated person, a Savior on a cross.

In *Reaching Out: The Three Movements of the Spiritual Life*, Nouwen describes the spiritual journey as relational in nature, featuring three prayerful movements toward wholeness: toward our truest self "inward," toward God "upward," and toward each other "outward." A journey of healing involves these three movements becoming integrated in a person's mental, physical, and spiritual life.[4]

The three movements can be understood as a series of polarities:

The journey into our innermost self is a movement from loneliness to solitude. Nouwen posits that we cannot be truly present to another unless we can first be present to ourselves. This movement takes us from anxious reaction to loving response.

The journey of reaching outward to our fellow human beings is a movement from hostility to hospitality. This requires vulnerability on our part to make room to receive people in unconditional love.

The journey of reaching out to God is a movement from illusion to prayer. It lies in the polarity of moving from the illusion that we are in control, masters of our own fate, into the ultimate reality of communication, trust, and reliance upon God.[5]

In each of these movements a person may encounter wounds that require healing: a God wound, in which we are hostile or resentful toward God; an inner wound, in which we cling to guilt, shame, or fear; or an outer wound, made of real or perceived harms that have been inflicted upon us by others. Coming to terms with these wounds requires vulnerability on our part. The honest confession of our own brokenness is our starting point toward a journey of reunification and wholeness.

In our outward movement toward others, therefore, Nouwen's concept of compassion encourages us to be weak with the weak, vulnerable with the vulnerable, and powerless with the powerless. Some have called this a "theology of weakness" or even a "spirituality of imperfection."

For Nouwen, the true Christian community is a place of hospitality, where people can welcome one another in grace and love in the fullness of their broken condition. This is not a community free of fear, loneliness, confusion, or pain, but a community in which suffering can be dealt with honestly and creatively. The focus is not the "curing" of wounds, but rather seeing them as openings for solidarity in our flawed condition. Every person is disabled in some way, whether physically, emotionally, or spiritually, because our "very good" creation (see Gen 1:31) has been fragmented by sin. Our theology of weakness forces us to acknowledge our dependency on God and one another. As we offer each other gratitude, encouragement, and hope in a circle dance of reciprocity, we become a community of healing for each other.[6]

Nouwen's best-known work, *The Wounded Healer*, powerfully resonates with many precisely because there are only wounded healers. There is no such thing as unwounded healers, particularly for those of us who are taking our cues from Jesus of Nazareth, the resurrected, ascended, and still-wound-bearing Lord (see John 20:25).

Nouwen embraced his own anguish, using it to bring healing to others. He painted with ashes. His life and work offer us a framework to become communities where wounded healers can learn to paint with ashes together.

The starting point is the acknowledgment that wounds are an expression of the brokenness of our shared human condition. We all have them. When it comes to brokenness, people typically have one of several defaults:

1. We go through life unaware we are broken.

2. We are aware of our brokenness but hide it from the world.

3. We are aware of our brokenness, go through an extensive (and often expensive) inner journey to find healing from it, and then hide it from the world.

4. We go through a process of healing our brokenness and then become experts who tell others how to heal.

5. We become aware of our own brokenness. We see it as the entry point to enter fully into our humanity and join others in a journey of graceful healing together.

This book is about embracing the fifth default: acknowledging that our greatest asset is in fact our greatest brokenness.

In the Bible, the book of Psalms is a powerful resource to assist us in our healing. The psalmists provide us an entire collection of poem-like prayers, called "laments," to help us journey through grieving. A lament gives us a vehicle to release the toxic infection of our wounds. Laments can also help us discover the truth of King David's admission to God: "if I make my bed in the depths, you are there" (Psalms 139:8). Pain is real, and yet God is somehow there with us in the midst of it. These are psalms in which honest anguish, deep distress, and heart-cry despair can be shared in community with others. As we will explore more fully later, healing begins when we articulate these emotions in an uncensored way.

When we share our brokenness with others, God does God's best work through us. This doesn't mean we go around spewing our woundedness upon others. Pain, trauma, and loss require an appropriate process of grieving. Untreated wounds keep us sick. As we say in recovery, "hurt people hurt people." But paradoxically, God uses wounded healers to heal other wounded people.

Weakness is transformed into superpower in a communal atmosphere of grace where people are free to be vulnerable.

We live in a world that is wounded and weeping. Our pace rarely gives space to grieve. But there is a wounded healer who longs to hold us in our tears. Healing takes place in safe conditions where honest stories of woundedness can be shared. Communities that are accessible, safe, and real can allow people to process their trauma in an unfiltered way. Cultivating these healing communities, where people can paint with ashes, can help heal the world.

Adam Brown paints with ashes in another way. The Missouri-based artist uses his painting skills to help ease the suffering of family members who have lost a loved one. He mixes ashes, the remains of the deceased, with paint pigments, and then uses this memorial palette to create portraits of the dead.

Brown said, "It hit me that having ashes in an urn on a fireplace would be a good way to remember that someone died, but having them in a piece of art is a good way of remembering that someone lived."[7] Our human instinct prompts us to hide our ashes in an urn and seal them away, to place them where only we know where they are. But what if by painting with ashes we can help others truly live and heal?

I first learned to paint with ashes in a juvenile detention facility. There, as an incarcerated teenage felon, I got "Thug 4 Life" tattooed on my arm. The ink was created from melted-down chess pieces. The ashes from the burnt plastic were collected and mixed with shampoo to create the makeshift ink. The artistic method of jailhouse tattooing with ashes is called "pick and poke." It involves taking a staple, sharpening it down to a needle, and then repeatedly piercing the skin to insert the ink. This tattooing method is an artistic innovation of incarceration culture. But do not try this at home. It is dangerous and painful!

After Jesus rescued me from that life and I became an ordained pastor, I decided "Thug 4 Life" was no longer representative of my vocational dream. Laser tattoo removal is a painful and expensive procedure. It takes many treatments to fade a piece even slightly. Cover-up tattooing, however, is a whole art form in itself. In a cover-up, you incorporate the old tattoo into a new one. The previous art doesn't go away but is integrated into the new creation.

The jailhouse "Thug 4 Life" tattoo on my arm has now been transformed into a lion and lamb portrait. The prophet Isaiah depicted the lion and the lamb as symbolic of the Messianic age and a coming peaceable kingdom (Isa 11:6). That in-breaking kingdom was embodied and inaugurated by Jesus, who is both the slain Lamb, who takes away the sins of the world (John 1:29) and the triumphant resurrected Lion, who has conquered death (Rev 5:5). In the skin on my arm remains the ash of jailhouse chess pieces, remixed now as a portrait of Jesus. Something that was once a mark of fallenness has become for me a symbol of grace, restoration, and new creation.

As told in the Scriptures, the prophet Jeremiah received a word from the Lord down at the potter's house. There he saw the potter working at the wheel. But the clay vessel he was forming became marred in his hand. Rather than scrapping the piece and discarding the hunk of clay, he "reworked it into another vessel, as seemed good to him" (Jer 18:2–6 NRSV).

This is the way God paints with ashes. God makes "all things new" by working with existing material (Rev 21:5 NRSV), taking what's marred and reworking it. God takes throwaways and gives them a new identity. God doesn't scrap the project and give up on us, no matter how seemingly ruined we become. By a transformative work of grace, God weaves our broken places into a beautiful mosaic. The wounds don't go away, but they are integrated into God's new creation. God takes the scars of our pain, and like a master cover-up tattoo artist, paints them into a masterpiece of grace.

God brings forth beauty from ashes by getting down into the grey soot of our wounds and painting our lives beautiful again. In doing so, God teaches us how to be artists of life and hope together. This book is an invitation for you to join a community of people learning to paint with ashes.

INTRODUCTION: THE DUNGEON FLAMED WITH LIGHT

"I was in prison, and you came to me."
—Jesus, in Matthew 25:36

I lay in a pool of blood on the floor of cell AC 222 in the Marion County Jail. That is Alpha Pod, C Section, solitary confinement cell 222, for those of you unfamiliar with the "MCJ" or incarceration-speak in general.

I was on the floor because it was no better or worse than the steel bunk with no mattress, sheets, or pillow. Also, because I was quite angry that my extended suicide attempt by way of alcohol and opioid narcotics had failed, and my brain was still a little foggy in my forced detox.

I heard the familiar sound of keys jingling and strong boots striking the ground. The racket stopped at my cell. A large black woman resembling Octavia Spencer as the momma-God in the film *The Shack*, knelt and looked through my chow slot. She laid a Bible in the slot, smiled, rose, and walked away. I never saw her again, even though I would spend many more days and months in that jail.

"What the fuck do you want me to do with that?" I shouted. "Why don't you get me a mattress?" The jingling keys and boots grew fainter and fainter until I was left in silence. My first impulse was to kick that Bible right back out of the chow slot. I raised my leg and was inches away from doing it. I can't honestly tell you why I didn't.

Maybe it reminded me of some shred of goodness in a former life. Childhood memories of carrying a lighter to light candles on the altar played in my head, along with echoes of Sunday school and the soundtrack to *The Prince of Egypt.*

I didn't want to think about those things. This is partly why I had been living in a blackout state in the years leading up to my arrest.

For some reason, I picked up that Bible. It had a silver hologram cover: New International Version, Youth Edition, illustrated with discussion questions. More memories I didn't want to think about. I took into serious consideration throwing that Bible against the wall, ripping the cover off, sliding it across the floor.

Then I thought to myself, *I'm probably going to be in here for a while, and I literally have nothing else to do.*

Earlier that day, I had gotten into an altercation with another inmate, which turned into an altercation with the guards who tried to break us up, which turned into a new arrest and being dragged down into the deepest dungeon of the jail. As my colleagues at the time described, solitary confinement was "jail in jail." Most people never come out the same.

The whole scene had been an attempt to establish myself as a badass, victimizing the weakest person I could find, so I could hide the fact I was a junkie going through massive withdrawals and didn't want to be in the general population. It was essentially another semi-calculated suicide attempt.

Prison officers don't like it when you fight them. They let me know this by slamming my face on the floor and getting in a few good licks before cuffing me and carrying me down to AC 222. They also conveniently neglected to leave me with a mat, blanket, sheets, or any other of the normal solitary confinement amenities.

I was in a bloodstained orange felony jumpsuit (the blood was mine), with no underwear (they only allow tighty-whities, and I had come in with colored boxer briefs) and no shoes. As I lay there, my friends back in general population were conveniently raiding my basket of any valuables, including the shoes I never had time to strap up.

As a normal resident with lots of frequent-flier miles at the MCJ, I knew I would never see those items again.

Initially the desire to throw the Bible at the wall or kick it out the door hole was overcome by sheer boredom. At some point, a day or two into what would become an extended stay in motel AC 222, I opened the Bible, and I started to read.

Over the next several days, I spewed diarrhea and puked stomach bile—sometimes simultaneously. And I read the NIV Youth Edition Study Bible. As I hallucinated, I relived every memory and felt every feeling I had been numbing with hundreds of milligrams of OxyContin every day. I read from Genesis to Revelation and memorized the list of the sixty-six books.

As I had flashbacks of violent altercations and exchanging sex with women who didn't have any money for the drugs I sold, I read about "male and female" created in the image of God and called "very good" (Gen 1:27, 31).

As the memories of waking up naked beside strangers with whole days and weeks missing in my memory, wondering what their names were and what crimes we had committed, I read about Jesus touching the lepers, healing the blind, and hanging with sinners, tax collectors, and prostitutes.

I thought about the small country of children I had spawned, how they would be taken from the harem of drug-addicted women I had left them with when I was arrested. How after the women ran out of drugs, they would probably sell those kids, or—best-case scenario—my kids would land in a Department of Children and Families foster home. Also, how I would have to get out and go through the custody process all over again.

I read the Psalms, memorizing some of my favorites: 1, 8, 23, 51, and 91. I can still recite them word for word today.

I begged God to give me just a minute's relief, as my muscles spasmed uncontrollably and I writhed in a living nightmare from which I could not wake up. The "just let me die" prayer was my daily companion.

I flashed back to carrying firearms, gang rivalries, and the heat of a bullet that had whizzed by my face. Then I read about a God who promised a new creation, where we would not know death or sickness, a place that would wipe away every tear from our eyes, a place where wolves and lambs would lie down together, and the nations would beat their swords into plowshares and their spears into pruning hooks and not make war anymore.

Eventually, the guards brought me a mat, a blanket, and a pillow. Even more generously, they brought me writing pads and a little rubber writing pen. Just enough of a pen to write a word, but not enough of one to turn into a weapon.

Even the biggest hard-ass among them must have felt pity for me. I rolled the mat up and stood it upright in the corner, where a single slit of sunlight shone through from outside. I sat with my face in the warmth of the light and read that Bible.

I wrote—a lot. I wrote about things I learned in the Bible. I wrote about memories from my childhood. I wrote letters to my girlfriends and my children. I wrote about dreams and visions I had, both sleeping and waking. I wrote stories. I wrote poems. I wrote my way out of the cell, transcending into a place of creativity, a womb of the Spirit, not bound by time or space.

You will never understand how generous God is with a single day until you are in a solitary confinement cell for forty-five straight days. With no external stimuli, no phone calls, rare showers, and infrequent recreation times in a cage outside each week, time can be your ally or your greatest enemy.

Abba Moses, fourth-century Ethiopian ascetic monk, notable among the Desert Fathers, said, "Go, sit in your cell, and your cell will teach you everything." I'm quite sure this was not what he had in mind.

I would count the days by the three trays that were placed in my chow slot. Breakfast tray. Lunch tray. Dinner tray. That's a day. In between was the reading of the hologram-covered NIV Youth Edition Study Bible, and the writing.

That's not to say each day was uneventful. Alpha pod, Charlie section, was reserved for the worst criminals. Murderers, rapists, cop fighters, and the mentally ill. Night and day, they banged on the doors and yelled, laughed, and taunted. Food, paper, and rubber pens were exchanged in an ingenious system of "fishing lines" made from strips of torn sheets, alternately confiscated and remade.

Some made a sport of storing up their feces and throwing it at the officers. Others made a racket until the CERT (Corrections Emergency Response Team) came in and gave them a fight. Some died in that hellish place with a sheet around their neck. Some were insane when they came in; they spent time strapped in a chair with a spit mask on. Others came in normal but, broken by time and solitude, left insane.

Humans are indeed social animals. Social animals don't do well in cages. We are created for relationship. Isolation can be a form of hell.

Me, I read the Bible. I wrote. Eventually, I sang, songs of faith I remembered from my childhood, old Methodist hymns (we people called Methodists sing our faith). I began to pray and talk to God. More important, I started listening to God.

That cell became a sanctuary. My cell was indeed teaching me. There, in the most severe possible human confinement that our society uses as a corrective measure, I went through withdrawal and discovered a new life. That is when my second life started, or perhaps my third or fourth.

I never saw that beautiful Octavia Spencer–like woman again, the one who had dropped the Bible in my slot like Momma God offering Mack milk and cookies in *The Shack*. I don't know who she was or where she came from or why she came into the AC, stopped at cell 222, placed a Bible in the chow slot, and smiled.

The Bible tells us of the importance of hospitality and notes that at times, we "have entertained angels unawares" (Heb 13:2 KJV). Call me superstitious, but I think she was an angel, a beautiful, black, cherub-faced messenger. She probably saved my life. She wasn't the only one, though. During those years, God loved to send angels in the form of green suits with handcuffs into my life.

One of the hymns I learned as a little boy in the neighborhood United Methodist congregation where I grew up was titled "And Can It Be?" and was written by Charles Wesley (1707–1788). Verse 4 reads:

Long my imprisoned spirit lay,
Fast bound in sin and nature's night;
Thine eye diffused a quick'ning ray—
I woke, the dungeon flamed with light;
My chains fell off, my heart was free,
I rose, went forth, and followed Thee.

This particular hymn gives me Holy Spirit chill bumps every time I sing it because it describes my experience of the risen Jesus. He came to me in a prison cell more than once to tell me I was beloved. He held me in his wounded hands, and wept over me as I pissed and shat myself going through withdrawals from opioid narcotics.

Jesus is the light that flamed in my dungeon.

I wish I could say that this little "dungeon flamed with light" experience was my last time being incarcerated, that I turned it all around and that life has been peaches and cream ever since. Only that wouldn't be true. There were more trips to the jail, more mistakes, and more moments of grace. Many more. The significance of that time was a spiritual turning point that took some time for me to grow into.

I wish I could say that I always believed what Jesus told me, that I was "beloved." But even now, I don't believe it some days. Don't get me wrong: it's the burning obsession of my life to help others believe that for themselves, but it remains much harder to embrace it for myself. The struggle is real, even today, right now, as I write these words.

Today when people look at me, they see a father, husband, pastor, professor, and author (albeit one with tattoos). It is true that I am all those things. They are pieces of my identity. But underneath who I am today is a twenty-year-old, scared little boy, bloodied on the floor of a solitary confinement cell. He lives in me too. I don't want to forget him. I visit him frequently. I peer through the slot and see him lying there in an orange felony jumpsuit, covered in his own mess. I go in and hold him and tell him it will be okay. Just don't kick the Bible out of the slot!

As you see, part of this book is about telling my story. That is, to the best of my ability, in the truest way possible, and in my own voice. (Considering the copious amounts of LSD, cocaine, marijuana, alcohol, Ecstasy, and opioid narcotics I used, this is no easy feat.) Part of my story includes how my higher power is unfolding a journey of healing in my life, and for me that higher power is Jesus.

However, my life cannot be articulated as a single story, shared in isolation from other stories. It would be like trying to understand the design of a tapestry by only reflecting on a single thread.

I will draw upon many stories from the great cloud of witnesses—people who painted with ashes across the ages. Archbishop Desmond Tutu is among them. Tutu struggled against apartheid in South Africa, a system of segregation and discrimination on grounds of race in which thousands of black people were harmed, imprisoned, and murdered. Even in the face of the continual threat to his own life, he persevered.

Tutu once spoke at a protest meeting in Cape Town, where just days earlier police had brutally killed two boys. Even with that trauma fresh in the minds and hearts of those gathered in that township, the archbishop remembers the moment when the crowd began to laugh. The gift of joy amid profound anguish made a lasting impact on him. He began to think deeply about the power of forgiveness.[1]

At the end of apartheid in the early 1990s, the newly elected president, Nelson Mandela, appointed Tutu to head the Truth and Reconciliation Commission (TRC), a task force charged with investigating apartheid-era crimes against humanity. The TRC engaged in a process of restorative justice in which survivors could receive reparations and confessing criminals could receive amnesty. Tutu's radical concept of forgiveness lay at the center of the approach. Archbishop Tutu believed that forgiveness was a fourfold process in which survivors needed to tell their story, name their hurt, grant forgiveness to the perpetrator, and then renew or release the relationship. The public TRC hearings brought together victimizers and victims to name their offenses, seek reconciliation, and facilitate forgiveness.[2]

Exactly this kind of forgiveness is required to paint with ashes. Forgiveness we give to God, ourselves, and even those who harmed us.

Undergirding Tutu's lifework on forgiveness and the TRC's approach to restorative justice is the African anthropological framework of *ubuntu*. The concept of *ubuntu* highlights the interdependency of humanity. All individuals are woven together in a single interconnected organism, so that even a small act of forgiveness impacts the entire world.

Ubuntu: a person is a person through other persons.

A simple way to understand *ubuntu* is by the phrase "a person is a person through other persons." One person's humanity is inextricably linked in a bundle of life with all others. Thus, to understand our story, we need to understand the larger story that we are a part of. We also need to understand that our story is a single strand of a much larger tapestry of creation. In some ways, when I tell my story, I tell your story, and I also tell our story. A universal cord resonates through the particularity of every life.[3]

This is what Henri Nouwen meant when he said, "For the minister is called to recognize the sufferings of his own time in his own heart and make that recognition the starting point of his service."[4] This is true of ministers, for sure. But it is also true of every single human being ever created. It is partly our broken condition that binds us together in a common humanity (Rom 3:23). When we can see that brokenness, when we know that it exists in every person we will ever meet, we can embrace a posture of *ubuntu*. We are who we are through others, and we need to be in relationship with those others in a way that brings healing to us all.

We all have wounds. We all have brokenness. We all need to give and receive forgiveness. We all have ashes. Not concealing the broken places can bring the most healing to us, others, organizations, communities, and as Tutu showed us, even entire nations. When our stories are shared, our pain named, forgiveness and the renewal of relationships are made possible.

The Africentric notion of self emphasizes personhood as a manifestation of community—a socially constructed self. A person's state of wellness is bound to a web of relationships. Connectedness, belonging, and social acceptance are emphasized rather than individuation. *Ubuntu* highlights *community* as the goal of life. Wounds are not created in isolation, they are created in community, and they can only truly be healed in community.

Every person is painting with ashes in some way.

Knowing this can help us receive and extend grace to others and give us courage to tell our stories. By hearing the stories of others, we learn how to live our own lives more fully. Sharing my story, and how it interacts with others, is done in hopes that it will help you more fully understand your story. Let's consider that God may be inviting us both to paint beside him with our ashes too. I can share my story because I have experienced other brave people sharing their stories. They showed me how they painted with ashes. Their stories healed me. They gave me courage to tell my own.

Ultimately, my hope for this book is that you will come to realize how much God loves you. Half my life I lived trapped in the chains of guilt and shame. Some days those feelings come back from the abyss like tentacles pulling me back into a bottomless pit. The shackles fell free for me the first time I heard God say, "I love you; you are my beloved; with you I am well pleased."

That release has taken many years, and it still goes on. More important, it has taken many stories. Years of listening to people tell their stories in the rooms of recovery fellowships helped me become comfortable enough to tell my own. I discovered that I was not "terminally unique" but that there was a whole sea of humanity that in many ways was just like me. They had done things just as crazy as I had, and even worse.

It turns out we all have "dungeons flamed with light" moments. They don't necessarily include a solitary confinement cell. For me, my life felt like a building that had burned to the ground, and no one had bothered to come rescue me. Somehow, I had survived the inferno, but the horror of the blaze had paralyzed me. For many years I sat there in the smoldering ashes, wiping the soot off my face, stuck in a never-ending "woe is me" lament. Then, some people came along and showed me how to paint with ashes, to take the smoldering ruins of my life and brush forth portraits of the beauty, truth, and goodness all around me in the world.

I hope you will learn to take your brokenness and use it in incredible, life-giving ways. I hope you will discover how your wounds can bring healing to others.

I hope you, too, can learn to paint with ashes.

PART ONE:
LOSS

1

BUTTERFLIES OF EDEN

*God saw all that he had made, and it was **very good**. And there was evening, and there was morning—the sixth day.*

Genesis 1:31 (emphasis mine)

"My mother left me, and I stayed behind in the Garden of Eden." This is how Itzchak Belfer described his entry into an orphanage at age seven.[1]

Belfer, who became a famous painter and sculptor, was born in April 1923 to a religious Jewish family in Warsaw, Poland, as one of six children. His father was a poor merchant and a leader in the local synagogue. He died when Belfer was only four. Belfer's mother struggled to provide for her children. In desperation, she took her son to live in the Warsaw orphanage.

As a child, Belfer had quite an imagination and enjoyed drawing. In the orphanage, he was provided paper, brushes, and paints, and was even given a little room of his own to paint in. He made the most of his time in that orphanage, describing the time as precious moments of happiness. It was there that he learned his love for art and started his career. Somehow, in these desperate circumstances, Belfer was able to make an inner journey to his own belovedness. He discovered, in spite of being an abandoned child and living at the orphanage for seven years, that he was a person of worth and sacred value, loved by God and others.[2]

His was no run-of-the-mill orphanage. This particular Warsaw orphanage, which Belfer described as his Edenic space, was run by a legendary man named Janusz Korczak. Korczak, who wrote under the pen name Henryk Goldszmit, was a Polish Jewish educator, children's author, and pedagogue. Most know of Korczak by the final courageous moments of his life. He marched hand and hand with the children of his orphanage and boarded a train heading for the Treblinka extermination camp. There, he and his little flock were murdered by the Nazis in 1942. Korczak willingly chose this fate rather than abandon the children he so dearly loved, many as gifted as little Itzchak.

Korczak's orphanage was a haven for hundreds of children. Also known as "the Doctor," Korczak empowered them with values of responsibility and respect. He established a functioning parliament, court, and newspaper in the orphanage, and each child had individual responsibilities to fulfill. Korczak believed that every child had value and needed an opportunity to learn, grow, and express himself or herself within a community of equals. Arguably, no one in history more thoughtfully described the plight of childhood abandonment and created a way to bring dignity and a chance of flourishing to children. To be a citizen of the Warsaw orphanage was to be adopted into a new family, and Korczak was the father.[3]

Korczak came from a well-to-do family. As a child, he was deeply impacted when he saw so many children his own age growing up in poverty and squalor. When Korczak was eleven, his father had a psychotic break and was hospitalized. His father died when Korczak was eighteen. Korczak knew firsthand what it was like to experience loss at a young age. Perhaps it was some fear of abandonment and the possibility of going mad that drove Korczak in his own work.[4]

Belfer left the Warsaw orphanage just before the Nazi invasion. He enjoyed a distinguished career as an artist, with much of his work preserving the treasured memories he had of Korczak. Many of his pieces bear Korczak's image, and his works have been displayed in numerous exhibitions both in Israel and internationally. One of his well-known sculptures stands in the city of Günzburg, Germany. It depicts Korczak surrounded by a group of his children.

In 2021, Belfer died in Tel Aviv at ninety-eight years old. He was the last living survivor of Korczak's orphanage. He sustained a spirit of deep joy and appreciation for his time there. He literally transformed what for some would be an insurmountable challenge into a vehicle for expressing transcendence in the world. Through his paintings and sculptures, he took the ashes of his childhood and painted the world more beautiful.

In Korczak's orphanage, Belfer found his "Garden of Eden" a place of innocence, protection, and nurture; a place where he was affirmed and encouraged to create and express his inner life in community with others.

≈≈≈⋙⋘≈≈≈

Maya Angelou (born Marguerite Ann Johnson, April 4, 1928) found her place of Eden in her grandmother's home in rural Stamps, Arkansas. After her parents' divorce, three-year-old Maya and her four-year-old brother, Bailey, were placed onboard a train with tags on their wrists that said, "To whom it may concern: Stamps, Arkansas, care of Annie Henderson." They were sent to a small, segregated town, where Maya was raised by her grandmother Annie, whom she called "Momma." There Maya was encouraged to read and study, which ultimately led her to become academically advanced compared to other children her age.

In Stamps, she was mentored by a well-educated woman named Bertha Flowers, who taught her the value of the spoken and written word. Bertha had Maya memorize and recite passages from the books she would loan her.

Like the orphanage for Belfer, Stamps became an Edenic place where Angelou felt safe and secure, a refuge of learning that gave her hope for the future. While she faced many great challenges throughout her lifetime, she carried her Edenic place with her in all her travels. Maya didn't allow her pain and abandonment to break her but used it to become a dancer, scholar, poet, memoirist, and civil rights activist.

Maya Angelou painted with ashes. She published seven autobiographies, three books of essays, and several books of poetry. In her creative work she was able to access a place of inner pain but use it to bring healing to others through her artistic expression. She is credited with a list of plays, movies, and television shows that spans more than fifty years. Among dozens of awards, the little girl raised by her grandmother in Stamps also received over fifty honorary degrees.[5]

I deeply resonate with Angelou's journey. In the early years of my childhood, my personal Eden was my grandparents' backyard. I, too, called my grandmother "Momma." Like many children from the crack epidemic of the 1980s, I was born addicted and was abandoned by my biological mother at birth. My biological father is … well, you'll see.

I was legally adopted by my grandparents. Grandpa was a World War II veteran who had experienced abuse and abandonment in his own childhood. My grandmother worked as an office administrator and then manager in the cafeteria of our local high school. My grandparents moved from New York City to settle in Ocala, Florida, in the late 1960s. Both provided for me and made sure I had the necessities of life, but neither was particularly affectionate or warm.

I spent a lot of time by myself, using my imagination to reshape the reality of my abandonment and isolation. The neighborhood boys used the hill in the front of our house as a bike ramp. They would subversively come racing by, hit the hill, fly into the air, and haul tail, laughing, down the road, as my grandpa ran cursing after them. That was the extent of my social interaction outside of school.

From my earliest memories, I was always launching into some entrepreneurial venture or another. I had a copper piggy bank with two of the legs broken off, replaced by simple screws. A great deal of my childhood life was consumed with filling the wounded, peg legged piggy with dollar bills and coins.

I was your run-of-the-mill child entrepreneur those first ten years. I did the standard enterprises: lemonade stands, raking leaves, and picking up pecans to save my grandpa's lawn mower blades (a quarter for every bag). At one point, I took up the somewhat unusual venture of caterpillar hunting. We had a small vegetable garden, an assortment of flowers, and banana trees in our backyard. During caterpillar season in Florida, anything green would be eaten alive by the caterpillars. My grandfather thoroughly indoctrinated me in the narrative that these hairy little worms were the enemy. I justified that their death was warranted and became an adept hunter. I would fear-lessly pluck them from any object and place them in empty peanut jars. My grandfather kept hundreds of these jars in his workshop, a small building that he built with his own hands in the back corner of our lot. I would pack these jars with caterpillars. They would crush each other in the sealed space, green caterpillar guts smearing the glass. I can still remember the smell of suffocating and deceased caterpillars when I would pop the lid off the jar.

The first time I brought Grandpa a couple of filled jars, I felt a sense of sorrow as he poured them into a basin of water and drowned them before my eyes. The sorrow was quickly overcome, though, by money as he placed a handful of coins in my hand, which I then dropped into Mr. Piggy. After that first time, he reduced his offer of a penny per caterpillar to a nickel per jar of caterpillars. I brought him hundreds of caterpillars at a time to be mercilessly drowned.

My expertise as the Steve Irwin of caterpillar hunting grew to include secret forays into the neighbor's yards as well. Who's to say those suckers wouldn't make their way to our backyard? After several seasons of this work, I learned a shortcut. The caterpillars would form cocoons in the trees. Over time those cocoons would be swollen fat with entire communities of caterpillars. Hundreds in a single location. I started finding ways to climb the trees and cut the cocoons free. I used a rope and pulley system to snatch them off the branch.

It was caterpillar genocide, really. I don't think I actually grasped the concept that caterpillars eventually metamorphosed into butterflies. I was focused on filling my bank. I'm surprised my grandpa was able to afford our deal, but he always honored his commitment of a nickel per jar.

Aside from caterpillar season, I found other ways to pack the piggy. I would make tickets, set up a stage in the backyard, and position stuffed animals as my audience. I would sell the tickets to my grandmother (my only live customer for many years), then put on shows with comedy, dancing, and acting. I created menus for a back-porch café (again, my grandmother was my only customer), where I served tea and cookies—provided, of course, by her. A dollar per show, sometimes multiple shows per week.

When that got boring, I started a church. I preached sermons while pacing back and forth on a stone wall that served as my stage and pulpit. I would carefully rehearse these gospel presentations, then invite my only church member (grandma again) to come and worship. At some point the collection plate would come out, and my one loyal church member would drop in her "tithe."

Later, I started my own publishing company of sorts. I made my own version of handwritten graphic novels on big sheets of paper folded over and stapled at the seam. I created illustrated stories, comic books, and adventure novels. After stapling the sheets together and creating a cover, complete with made-up ISBNs, I sold these books to my only customer (again, my grandmother).

Grandpa had had his own home décor and yard ornament business back in New York City. He was the kind of man who could build anything. Alongside his workshop in our backyard, he also built a small home for my great-grandmother to live in. We called it "the bungalow." Grandpa built that two-bedroom, one-bathroom bungalow from the ground up. He was an amazing craftsman, proficient in masonry, carpentry, plumbing, electrical wiring, and essentially anything else. I remember following him around trying to help with projects, carrying his tools, and holding his nails. It seemed to be one of the only ways I could connect with him. He didn't talk or show affection, so joining him in projects made me feel close to him, and I enjoyed learning how to build stuff, which was great fun.

It seems I was a bit too effeminate for Grandpa, though. At times, he called me names, like "sissy" and "faggot." He was not amused by some of my more flamboyant theatrics in shows, sermons, and dance routines. This caused a creeping suspicion in my soul that something was defective about me. Also, it normalized for me that people who love us also harm us. As an adult, I realize his words wounded me, and to this day I struggle with forming deep relationships with other men.

Grandpa was the epitome of masculinity and warrior strength. Soldiers like him were not supposed to show emotion. My great-grandmother Edith lived in her bungalow until she died at 103. When she died, Grandpa was devastated. I saw him cry for the first and only time at her funeral. He said, "Goodbye, Momma" through his tears.

My biggest entrepreneurial venture in those days was the creation of my own amusement park. After a trip to Disney World in Orlando, I was inspired to create my own version right there at 812 Northeast Ninth Avenue in Ocala, Florida. Grandpa's extensive workshop materials provided everything I needed: wooden sawhorses, hundreds of empty milk crates, pipes, aluminum sheets, blocks, buckets, many of his yard ornament pieces, and fake stone creations.

The backyard was a veritable treasure trove of old tools, supplies, and building materials of various kinds. I began the normal process of innovation, rearranging those materials in new and creative ways. I turned my monkey bars into a kind of monorail system and built a wheelbarrow roller coaster. Stacks of milk crates became a climbable tower. Ropes crisscrossed the air between trees as a kind of zip line system. Those were some of the key attractions.

I designed the entire theme park from scratch, mapping out how visitors would move from one attraction to the next. I progressed from "Bunyon's Bridge" to the rope swing with a ninja turtle (me in a Michelangelo turtle mask with nunchucks); then I rode in the milk crate train safari, which ended in a real wooden slide. I climbed the stone wall beset by crocodiles that led to a stage where I provided an epic Indiana Jones–style enactment, going on finally to a "meet the characters space" (again personated by me, disguised as Dick Tracy, the detective).

After weeks of mapping out the space, designing the rides, and creating the flow (I would serve as the tour guide), I drew up some fliers. I went down to the homes where a couple of neighborhood kids lived and invited them to come check out my park, which I told them would open Saturday at 9:00 a.m. The cost was only a dollar—much more reasonable than Disney World or Busch Gardens! I handed some kids the fliers directly, while others I left on front doors.

The big day came. I dressed up like Indiana Jones, ready to host the crowds of neighborhood customers coming through the park.

My dog, Rambo, was my assistant. The day passed by slowly. No one came. Finally, I resorted to leading my stuffed animals through the adventure, along with Rambo, who seemed to enjoy it very much. At the end of the day, my only paying customer was . . . again . . . my grandmother.

Yet, at no time in my childhood can I remember feeling a sense of failure about all this. I was buoyed by the sheer joy of creating, the excitement of putting things together. The imagining and planning were energizing. Even if only my stuffed animals enjoyed the result, I never felt discouraged or exhausted.

Today, one of my roles is local church pastor. As with any endeavor, some in the church world analyze effort using mathematical means. It is not lost on me as a minister that institutional metrics only measure statistics: who shows up, how many, and how much they give. I wonder if this is something that gets educated into us in school. In *Think Like a 5 Year Old*, my friend Len Wilson describes this documented phenomenon as the "Fourth Grade Slump," the time when children become aware of their peers, which leads to dynamics of power. Kids' interests shift from the joy of creating to the satisfaction of finding approval through others.[6]

Interestingly, in the church world, too, we inhabit a system that encourages the seeking of approval but diminishes the joy of creativity. Success and failure measure who consumes what you create but ignore the process of creation.

This is in part what Jesus meant when he said, "Unless you change and become like children, you will never enter the kingdom of heaven" (Matt 18:3). Recovery from sin and all the isms of its aftermath includes rediscovering our childhood superpower of untamed imagination.

My grandparents' backyard was a kind of Eden for me, a place where I learned to hone my creative prowess. Even in my selfish quest to ruthlessly slaughter all the caterpillars to fill my piggy bank, somehow butterflies survived and flew freely there.

Contrary to so much fundamentalist Christian teaching about original sin, a Christian doctrine highlighting the bankrupt nature of our human condition from birth, in the Bible the starting point of our story is "very good." Everything that is, God creates out of his own Word and will and calls it good. God creates human beings, male and female, in the image of God, and calls the whole masterpiece *very good* (Gen 1:31).

For an Anglican cleric living in eighteenth-century England, *very goodness* was the starting point to understand God and humanity. John Wesley, and the Wesleyan theological position that bears his name, reminds us that this goodness precedes any business about being irreparably bad. Original sin is a way to talk about the current fragmented condition of the human race.

In a journey toward healing, if we don't get the starting point right, we can end up on the wrong path. If we are irrevocably bad and powerless to change, not much of a response is required on our part. We are born bad, stuck helplessly bad, and salvation is collapsed into being rescued and "going to heaven when we die" if we can just recite the correct creedal formula. But the biblical idea of "salvation" is much more expansive than this.

Jesus' name literally means "he who saves." The Greek word used to describe how Jesus will "save his people from their sins" is σῴζω (*sōzō*) (Matt 1:21). To "save" is not only about rescue or erasing penalties on a divine score card. It also denotes relief from suffering, healing from disease, or to make well, whole, and restore to health. The biblical vision of *shalom* (a world at peace) is much more expansive than saving souls for relocation to heaven when they die. It's about God's kingdom breaking into the world now. It's about the healing, renewal, and well-being of the entire cosmos. It's a holistic vision of God's reign on earth.

Salvation is a journey of restorative healing that requires our ongoing response.

Wesleyan theology, or "practical divinity," emphasizes waves of grace and a journey of transformation that begins in this life and continues into the next. God's first word to us is "you are my beloved, with whom I'm well pleased." We were once "very good," but through sin became wounded and in need of healing. Now, through a relationship with Jesus, we can be restored to our original goodness and find healing in this life.

It's quite remarkable that the starting point for Wesley's understanding of humanity emphasizes this *very goodness*, considering the *very broken* world in which it was developed.

The Methodist movement, which Wesley led, sprang to life in a society plagued by immense poverty, suffering, and evil. Wesley was a priest amid one of the worst crime waves in English history, a time of massive inequality, exploitation, alcoholism, and prostitution. The masses viewed the church with skepticism and associated it with overall corruption.

Wesley had his own wounds to contend with. He documented his spiritual convulsions in his journals. He was plagued with a sense of doubt and not-enoughness and questioned his own salvation regularly. Yet it was this upheaval in his own soul that drove him to lead a movement that changed the world.

After a meticulous effort to live an upstanding religious life, and a failed attempt to be a missionary to the newly forming American colonies, Wesley had a conversion experience on Aldersgate Street in London on May 24, 1738. There, someone read from Martin Luther's preface to Paul's letter to the Romans about the nature of being *saved by grace through faith*. The understanding that Wesley had in his mind, made the long journey into his heart. He described the experience as feeling his heart "strangely warmed."[7]

This was a formational event that set Wesley on a new spiritual course. Yet a close reading of his journal conveys that he still struggled spiritually following the Aldersgate experience. Wesley felt a powerful call to those unreached by the existing church. He was heavily criticized for his outward-oriented fervor, and many churches closed their doors in his face. His ministry became one primarily with those outside the church.

On April 2, 1739, at the compulsion of his friend George White-field, Wesley took up the "vile" practice of field preaching.[8] Preaching outside of a church sanctuary was highly frowned upon by the religious establishment. Yet, from that point, a transformation occurred in Wesley's spiritual life, documented by a marked change in the nature of his journal entries. For Wesley, the movement inward to his truest self and upward toward God was not complete until it had moved outward to others. The lifelong journey of grace is about growing in love for God and neighbor.

The people called Methodists worked against political corruption. They structured a systematic distribution of food, medicine, clothing, and loans. They organized jobs for the unemployed, educated orphans, and secured shelter for the homeless. Methodist gatherings were places where people of all walks of life came together as one.

Those first communities were places of embodied hospitality. They were places of healing that were *accessible*, *safe*, and *real*. Let's take a look at these three words.

- Accessible: The communities were formed in the normal spaces where people gathered, and spoke what has been described as "plain truth for plain people." The only requirement for membership was "a desire to flee the wrath to come."

- Safe: The communities met in smaller, intimate groups. All people from every social status were welcome, and harmful behaviors were not tolerated.

- Real: People were invited to come to terms with and express their brokenness. Methodist small groups asked, "How goes it with your soul?" People were invited to name their woundedness in a community of reciprocity and mutual support.

The Wesleyan way of "salvation" is a vision of holistic healing that takes place in community, begins in this life, and continues in the next. This starts from the utter conviction of the goodness of humanity, but also holds in tension our current brokenness.

Our human story begins in the goodness of a garden around a tree of life (Gen 2:9). The garden is an important place. Life starts in the garden of creation, with the first humans walking with God in the cool of the day (3:8). Life gets reset in another garden, one of flower-covered graves—a cemetery with an empty tomb (see John 20). Life continues eternally in an urban garden, where we once again gather at the tree of life (Rev 22:1–5).

There was only one restriction in that first garden paradise: don't eat from the other tree, the "tree of the knowledge of good and evil" (Gen 2:16–17). God gives us the gift of free will. We can choose to follow directions, or not. Of course, we chose the latter and turned utopia into a dystopia, something we have become quite experienced in doing throughout the ages. In our rebellion against God, sin, death, and evil enter the equation.

The first portrait of God after this "fall" is a loving God immediately seeking us out with the graceful call, "Where are you?" (Gen 3:9). God has been calling out "Where are you?" over us ever since. Our free will characterizes all creatures and things and can be used for good or ill. God has built into creation a certain kind of vulnerability. We do not just helplessly participate in a predetermined universe, but we can interact and shape what it becomes. So, free will opens possibilities, both good and bad. We can clearly see there is an element of randomness to the universe.

Many of our conceptions of God are tyrannical, a micromanaging God ruling over the universe in a deterministic fashion. In this view, God sits on a cloud, zapping people from on high, deciding this person will die in an accident today, that person will get cancer, or this baby will be born with his organs outside his body. But the Bible reveals a different God, one who is shaping a world with divine purposes and possibilities. Humans can use their own creative potential to heal or harm what is taking shape. So, "sin" is not simply rebellion against God but against creation.

Profound goodness, beauty, and truth are baked into us and God's "very good" creation. These are the ingredients with which we and the universe are made, yet those ingredients are currently corrupted. Not only does humanity need healing; so does creation itself (Rom 8:22). Death, disease, and natural disasters (natural evil), as well as human evil flourishing in individuals, institutions, and systems (moral evil) are obvious features of our current fragmented cosmos.

Painting with ashes requires us to understand where we fit into this larger story. We begin with the "very good" nature of God's creation, in which human beings are supremely good among all created things (Gen 1:27–31), and knowing that *very goodness* is still a possibility now and in the ultimate destination (Revelation 22). But we acknowledge that this truth is paradoxical, for pain, struggle, loss, and death, are enduring realities. We all find ourselves sitting in the ashes from time to time.

Many who have learned to paint with ashes first had to rediscover their inner Garden of Eden.

This involves the movement that Nouwen spoke of as a journey to our inner self. The process of healing is fundamentally a "recovery" of something that was lost. Becoming a "new creation" in Christ is not about *brand spanking new*, which is the obsession of an age typified by consumerism and waste. It's about something being renewed, healed, and restored to former goodness. The masterpiece is already inside us. Sometimes we just need to invite God to clean off the mess obscuring the surface.

Inside every caterpillar is a butterfly. The creature is the same in genetic and molecular substance but achieves a new state of being. It is the messy liquification and reconstitution process of metamorphosis that reveals the creature's true form. This is true of humans as well.

Somewhere in the course of our lives, there is an Eden, a place of innocence, where union with God, and "walking with God in the cool of the day" is the norm. A space where we have access to the tree of life. We all have one; some of us just need to look harder to find it. But then for everyone one of us there is a fall.

Itzchak's Garden of Eden was destroyed when his beloved doctor boarded a train with the children he had given his life for, heading for an extermination camp.

Maya Angelou's father showed up at Grandma's house in Stamps when she was seven and took her and her brother up to St. Louis, Missouri, to drop them off to live with their mother, Vivian. During that brief stay, Maya was raped by her mother's boyfriend, Freeman.

Under fear of his threat to kill her brother, Bailey, she intended to hide the rape. But because she was bedridden and bleeding for several days, her mother discovered the abuse. Freeman was arrested, Maya testified at his trial, and he was sentenced to prison. Before he could get carted off to the jail, he was assaulted and stomped to death in a vacant lot. Maya felt that her court testimony had led to his death. She went into a period of silence for five years and carried feelings of guilt for the murder of her attacker. She returned to her grandmother's house in Stamps, but she carried the trauma of her abandonment, abuse, and pain the rest of her life. Her Eden had been destroyed.

My Eden was destroyed too, in my grandparents' backyard when I was just ten, the details of which I will share in the pages to come. That was the beginning of my "fall," which would ultimately lead to darkness, alcoholism, cocaine addiction, arrest, and imprisonment. It was in that backyard that I ate from my own personal tree of knowledge of good and evil. It was there that I "died" and my innocence was lost.

2

GIFT OF DESPERATION

And not only that, but we also boast in our sufferings, knowing that suffering produces endurance, and endurance produces character, and character produces hope, and hope does not disappoint us, because God's love has been poured into our hearts through the Holy Spirit that has been given to us.
Romans 5:3–5 NRSV

Talk about a fall that couldn't get any worse. Here he was, a shell of a man, wasted away, barely a hundred pounds. William's body shook uncontrollably from the delirium tremens of withdrawal as he drifted in and out of a hallucinatory state. He had burned every bridge, failed at every business venture, and his marriage was in shambles. Now committed for alcoholic insanity for a third time, death or permanent institutionalization seemed like the only choices he had left. Yet in the desperation, a spark of hope glimmered. From the ashes, a seedling of new life emerged. This mess of a man would become a key instrument in saving millions of lives.

Alcohol prohibition began on January 16, 1920, when the Eighteenth Amendment went into effect. Federal Prohibition agents were given the impossible task of enforcing this new law. Due to the new restrictions, alcohol consumption went underground. Even though technically the sale of alcohol was illegal, "speakeasies" and other underground drinking establishments sprang up across the country, and "home brewing" became a new American pastime.

In the post-Prohibition 1930s United States, alcoholism soared to new heights. The common perception was that alcoholism was a moral failing. Medical treatment of the condition was primitive. The poor were only able to find help through the state's hospital systems. The Salvation Army and other religious organizations, such as the Oxford Group, tried to offer help, as well. Psychiatrists treated alcoholics with barbiturates and belladonna, or what was called the "purge and puke" method. Many severe alcoholics were committed to asylums.

In 1934, Dr. William D. Silkworth was the medical director of Towns Hospital in New York City. He worked on the front lines of this social and medical epidemic. Not only did everyday people die by the thousands, but lists of public figures and celebrity authors, actors, athletes, and musicians were dying from the disease as well: Hank Williams, Curly Howard, Sinclair Lewis, W. C. Fields, Lorenz Hart, John Barrymore, and Helen Morgan, to name a few.

Silkworth discovered that the "problem" of alcoholism was centered in the mind, manifesting as an "allergy" that unleashed a "phenomenon of craving." It was not merely a moral issue but a medical one. Once an alcoholic took a single drink, the "allergy" was agitated and unleashed. Silkworth's conventional treatments seemed helpless against the phenomenon.

One day, he encountered an anomaly, a patient of the most extreme variety, whom he had personally treated on multiple failed occasions. The patient had seemingly recovered from a hopeless state of mind and body and was helping other alcoholics recover through a rapidly growing grassroots fellowship.[1] Based on his observation of this remarkable patient, Silkworth wrote, "Unless this person can experience an entire psychic change there is very little hope of recovery," adding that the new ideals of the individual must be grounded in a "power greater than themselves."[2]

The individual he treated was Bill W., cofounder of Alcoholics Anonymous, a now global fellowship of over two million people encompassing more than 118,000 groups in 180 nations around the world.[3]

Bill W., whose formal name was William G. Wilson, was born on November 26, 1895, in East Dorset, Vermont. His paternal grandfather was an alcoholic but had a religious experience that led him to stop drinking. Bill's biological parents abandoned him not long after his sister and he were born. Dad went out of town for a business trip and never came back. Mom left to study osteopathic medicine, also never returning. Bill and his sister were raised by their maternal grandparents.

Bill married his wife, Lois, on January 24, 1918. Not long after the wedding, he departed to serve in World War I as a second lieutenant in the Coast Artillery. After Bill completed his military service, he and Lois lived in New York, where he made a failed attempt at law school. He then took to Wall Street as a stock speculator, but the drinking that had begun during military training grew progressively worse. In a flash of alcohol-inspired genius, he packed up Lois and went out on the road. The Wilsons traveled the United States, evaluating companies for potential investors. After a time of some success, Bill's drinking progressed to the point at which he was unemployable.

In 1933 Wilson was committed to the Charles B. Towns Hospital, where he came under the care of Dr. Silkworth for the first time. After three more hospitalizations, Bill realized that he would be permanently committed with "wet brain" or die.

After a visit from an old drinking buddy who had turned sober, Ebby Thacher, Bill saw that sobriety was a possibility and acknowledged a spiritual awakening of some kind. Bill remembered a transcendent moment he'd experienced many years earlier in a cathedral in Europe during the war. Ebby had found sobriety through the evangelical Christian Oxford Group. Bill began attending. (He and his AA cofounder would later adapt this program into the well-known "Twelve Steps.")

After a final bender, Bill was admitted back into Dr. Silkworth's care at Towns Hospital for the fourth time. Here, following a case of delirium tremens and the belladonna cure, Bill experienced a spiritual awakening that he would later refer to as his "White Light" experience. He was reborn.

Bill had been sober for about five months when he traveled to Akron, Ohio, for a shareholders' meeting and proxy fight. The meeting didn't go well, and he had a near relapse in a bar in the Mayflower Hotel, where he was staying. In that moment of desperation, he decided he needed to find another alcoholic, and quick. Bill called various people and was eventually introduced to an Akron surgeon, who had struggled for years with his own alcoholism.

That individual, Robert Holbrook Smith, would become known as simply "Dr. Bob." A physician and surgeon, Dr. Bob cofounded Alcoholics Anonymous (AA) with Bill. The two men held their first meeting on May 12, 1935, in Akron. Bill maintained sobriety from alcohol until his death in 1971. In 1999 *Time* magazine listed him as "Bill W.: The Healer," in "*Time* 100: The Most Important People of the Century."[4]

Bill W. was indeed "the healer"—a wounded healer. He was able to turn his worst challenge into an instrument of healing for others on a massive scale. He devoted his life to this new work. His deepest source of pain, frustration, and brokenness became the very vehicle for his vocation as a healer of other alcoholic souls. Bill W. painted with ashes.

The organization he cofounded has saved millions of lives from the grip of alcoholism. AA has spawned multiple other 12-step fellowships that have saved countless more from drug addiction, sex addiction, codependency, gambling, and other afflictions. Alcoholic Anonymous seems to have an answer to the age-old problem of alcoholism. This thriving global, leaderless, lifesaving organization is founded on some remarkably simple principles. These principles are crystallized in the collective intelligence of AA members everywhere in the form of recovery fellowship clichés.

One of the primary cliches is an acronym for God: *Gift of Desperation*. As Silkworth discovered, the treatment for the disease of alcoholism was spiritual in nature, and if an alcoholic didn't find the "gift of desperation," chances of recovery were unlikely. It was in the pit of institutionalization and near death that Bill found this gift. One of the key principles of the program is that nothing ensures long-term sobriety like intensive work with other alcoholics. Another cliché is "You need to give it away to keep it." When all else failed, Bill and Bob found help for themselves by helping other struggling alcoholics.

In the program, alcoholics learn a new set of behaviors: praying, going to meetings, talking to a sponsor, reading the *Big Book*, and making coffee. As we "fake it till we make it," we live ourselves into a new mindset, an entire "psychic change."[5] The Twelve Steps are a framework used to facilitate this entire psychic change.

Step 1 is an acknowledgment of desperation: *We admitted that we were powerless over alcohol—that our lives had become unmanageable.*[6]

In Genesis 3, the "fall" is about our conscious choice not to trust God. This causes a breach in our relationships with God, ourselves, and one another. It is in this context that desperation enters the human experience. We are forcibly thrust from our Garden of Eden. We lose access to the tree of life. No longer can we access God directly and have our daily chats in the cool of the day.

As nightmarish as this scenario seems, it is all for our own good. If we were to eat of the tree of life, we would continue on in some undead, zombielike, less-than–"very good" state. The whole Bible is the story of God calling out, "Where are you?" God is seeking to put what was lost and broken back together. God's redemptive, healing work of new creation is how God paints with ashes. Like a potter at the wheel, God is taking a vessel that has become marred, reworking it, and re-creating it anew (see Jer 18:1–10). In the fullness of time, God enters fully into our desperation to meet us in the midst of it (Gal 4:4).

While God does not will or cause our suffering, God is with us in the midst of it. "Somehow," as bad as it stings at the time, our desperation is a gift. It gives us lots of ashes to paint with. The stories we explore in this book are of those who turned their suffering into the driving force for their empathy and compassion. In the crucible of pain, our character and vocations are formed.

Another AA cliché is "pain is the touchstone of progress." Yet this is not a truth many people want to embrace. Perhaps this is why we abbreviate Reinhold Niebuhr's masterpiece now called the "Serenity Prayer." First, consider the whole prayer as originally composed by Niebuhr:

> *God, give us grace to accept with serenity*
> *the things that cannot be changed,*

courage to change the things
which should be changed
and the wisdom to distinguish
one from the other.
Living one day at a time,
enjoying one moment at a time,
accepting hardship as a pathway to peace,
taking, as Jesus did,
this sinful world as it is,
not as I would have it,
trusting that You will make all things right,
if I surrender to Your will,
so that I may be reasonably happy in this life,
and supremely happy with You forever in the next.
Amen.[7]

To live "one day at a time" and to accept "hardships as the pathway to peace" is the way of the wounded healer, Jesus, who by his wounds brought healing to us all (Isaiah 53). Persevering through pain not only forms us; it teaches us to have hope. For in trust and surrender we discover we are being held by God, a God with us (Matt 1:21–23). Only here can we learn the power of true joy—a joy that is an inside job, not dependent on external circumstances, but found in an abiding relationship with God. The world can't give this joy, and the world can't take it away. This results from the love God has "poured into our hearts through the Holy Spirit" (Rom 5:5).

It is in desperation that we learn the giver is the gift (Luke 11:13).

Ubuntu: we are people through other persons. My own life has been profoundly shaped by Bill W. and the various 12-step fellowships that resulted from his G.O.D. experience. This discovery of being sought, found, and held in a great moment of desperation can vary in degrees. Desperation can be a house with many basements, and some of us have to explore all the way to the bottom floor.

〜〜〜〜〜〜〜〜

While my own alcoholism started young, it would take many decades for me to receive that "gift of desperation."

During my childhood, my mom would come and crash at my grandparents' place occasionally. Each time she visited was both confusing and exciting. After my great-grandma Edith died, my mom moved into the bungalow with her husband. They had a child together, my little half brother, McKinley.

One day, I stood at the side door of my grandparents' house, looking back into the open door of the bungalow. My mom, her husband, and little brother seemed like a happy little family, talking and laughing together. That was probably the first time I remember a clear feeling of something being wrong with me. Why wasn't I part of that family? Why did my mom want McKinley but not me? Was I defective or something? Today I know that feeling as *shame*.

I would sneak around, listening to my mom talk, feeling quite awkward about eavesdropping, but driven by my curiosity to understand her. I eventually snuck into their bungalow. I could hear my brother crying in his crib. I looked down on him, screaming and writhing, and I felt a strong feeling of hatred toward him. It was the first time I can remember vile darkness coming out of my heart. I thought about smothering him. Suddenly my mother was there and yelled at me to get back, as though she could sense the malice in my soul. I ran back into my grandparents' home and cried.

The whole situation was confusing. My mom and her new family left, and I stayed behind.

Things were quiet for a few years, but one night my mother called on the phone and wanted to speak with me. For some reason, my grandmother took pictures of the moment on her Polaroid camera. She wrote on the back of one picture, "Michael talking to his mother." In the photo, I'm standing in Scooby-Doo pajamas, talking on a corded dial phone.

On the other end, my mother was telling me about her newfound life. She had gotten clean and sober, and she and her husband had a two-story house in New York City. The thing I remember the most was her telling me there was an arcade game in the basement. Mom wanted me to come and live with her new husband and my little brother, McKinley. She told me how I would love the city and could play the arcade game anytime. She made many other promises, but the adventure of the city and the all-access invitation to my own big-box arcade game were most compelling.

There was nothing wrong with my life with Grandpa and Grandma. I had a bit of a sweet deal. It was truly Edenic. I was fed, clothed, and provided for. But the overwhelming curiosity to know my mother proved stronger. I hung up the phone and said, "I want to go live with her for a while."

As I said those words, my grandmother broke down, sobbing. She yelled at my grandfather, and they fought it out for the rest of the night. They tried to convince me that I should not go. But I was motivated by the day I had stood by the side door, looking at my mom's bungalow.

Another Polaroid snapshot, this one with my grandmother's handwriting on the back: "Mikey flies to NYC to live with his mother." I remember holding my teddy bear, with his hand-sewn camouflage pants and G.I. Joe T-shirt; looking out a plane window; and seeing all the little homes and landscapes that looked like Play-Doh below.

Shortly after arriving in New York, I knew I had made a big mistake. My mother showered me with kisses and hugs, but her husband let me know immediately he did not want me there disturbing their happy little family. The night I arrived, my mom showed me the big-box arcade game in the basement. However, he told me I was never to play that game unless I had his permission . . . ever.

The second night there was a lot of drinking, followed by a drunken brawl. This was the first time of many I watched my mother get beat senseless by this huge bear of a man. I was frozen with terror and could not speak or act. This also made me feel like a coward.

I discovered that my mother's husband had four favorite pastimes: getting drunk and high, beating the hell out of her, abusing me, and threatening to kill us both if we told.

This ritual of drunkenness and beating was repeated almost nightly. I passed the days playing with my little brother, McKinley. Sometimes we used our imaginations to drown out the screams and the beatings and the crashes. Imagination really is a superpower.

My stepdad smelled like alcohol and cigarettes intermingled with cheap musky cologne. It wasn't long before I too had become a dartboard for his alcohol-induced rage. At one drunken party where a large group of people crowded into the house, he pulled down my pants, lifted me up in the air, and paraded me around the gathering as everyone laughed at me. More shame.

On several occasions, to make up for what he was doing to my mother and now to me, he would let me play the arcade game. He also took me to work with him at the shop where he was a mechanic. On one of those occasions, when he was feeling particularly cruel, after I cut myself trying to help him with a brake job, he tricked me into washing my hands in a pan of gasoline.

I went to an elementary school in New York City, of which I only have fleeting memories. However, I do remember sitting in an art class. We were given a coloring sheet of an apple and told to color it in. I started with red. Then added green. Then added blue. Then added yellow. Then added black. My "picture" ended up being a mass of darkness, obscuring the apple outline underneath. My teacher looked at my picture and asked what I had done. I looked around at the other students nearby, all who had colored beautifully within the lines, lots of typical red apples, brown stems, and green leaves.

My teacher could somehow see that my art was an expression of what was going on in my soul. Perhaps this is universally true of all of us: our art reveals what is going on inside us. In this case, she was so concerned that she sent me to the guidance counselor. There was suspicion that I was mentally handicapped in some way. My mother was called in to talk about what to do with me.

The first time I stood up to my mother being mercilessly beaten, I put myself in the middle of the fray and ended up getting thrown down the stairs. This necessitated a trip to the hospital for a broken arm. There was a massive fight between my mother and her husband about his "putting his hands on" me, followed by the big make up session.

We came home from the hospital, packed up our stuff furiously, and left the city, driving further into the frozen north. The place we ended up was Elmira, New York. It seemed to snow year-round. There was not much there but mountains and mobile home parks. Still, my stepfather was a top-notch mechanic and could always find work.

My aunt lived close by, and I remember meeting my two cousins, one of whom I had a crush on. My aunt was fifteen years older than my mother, and she seemed like a safe and maternal figure. But she also wrestled with her own demons.

My mother had some struggles of her own. In the summertime, when school was out, she would take us around from house to house while her husband was at work. My little brother and I would sit in the car, sometimes for long periods, as my mother went in to visit with her boyfriends. Many times, these men would come out in bathrobes to see her to the car, where McKinley and I would be waiting. Of course, this activity perpetuated the cycle of violence with my stepfather.

A great moment of desperation occurred when my stepfather took me on a snowmobile ride into the woods. We went deep back into the wild, where the snow was falling heavily. Once we got to a remote place, we stopped, and he told me to get off. I remember refusing and clinging to him for dear life. It's ironic that I was clinging to my abuser, who was also my only hope to live. He pushed me off of him and rode off into the distance.

The sun was setting. It was very cold and getting dark, and I could hear animals scurrying around. All I could do was stand still in the place where he left me. I held on to some hope that maybe it was all one of his sick games and he would come back if I just waited. Darkness fell, and the moonlight was the only source of light. I stood there, silently. Snow was piling up around me. As I began to explore the possibility of trying to find my way back, I could hear the buzzing of a snowmobile in the distance. Then I saw a light. My stepfather, under the influence of my mom, came back looking for me. I screamed and screamed, "Over here! I'm over here!" again and again. I had stood in the same spot where he had left me earlier in the day. My mother took me in her arms and said, "I'm so sorry, baby boy." Her husband drove me home, but I remember thinking to myself, *This man just tried to kill me.* I knew I was not safe.

After several failed attempts to run away, I accidentally got my wish. The next time I intervened on my mother's behalf, her husband punched me in the head, causing me to fall backward. I landed on the sharp edge of a Tonka truck, which required another trip to the hospital, for stitches. The medical staff asked me what had happened, and this time I told them. The next thing I remember is staying in a home with other children for several days until my grandparents arrived. They took me back to Florida, and I never considered living with my mother again.

I was grateful for life back at my grandparents' house. Compared to the hell I had experienced with my mother, I had stability and provision. One of my favorite pastimes became running around naked in our backyard in the rain. I would strip down and run around in thunderstorms, trying to catch rainwater in my mouth. My audience of one was always sitting on the back porch, watching.

How do we lose that? The wild abandon to run naked though thunderstorms?

When I was nine, my grandfather became sick. It was cancer. He died a year later. The last time I saw him in the hospital, I could hear the wheezing and mechanical sounds of impending death. It sounded like Darth Vader's durasteel, obsidian-colored bio-armor malfunctioning. I heard Gram call it the "death rattle." At Grandpa's funeral, I leaned over his casket and said, "Goodbye, Grandpa."

My mother and my aunt both came to the funeral. They took me out into the backyard and told me that Grandpa had molested and raped them both, and that he was my father. I was ten. That was the end of my Eden, the safe place where I'd learned to play, imagine, write, hustle, and pack the piggy.

My grandmother never quite recovered from losing Grandpa. She seemed kind of dazed and fatigued from that day forward. A couple of weeks after the funeral, she ran a stop sign. I could see the oncoming car barreling into my passenger door in slow motion. Time seemed to pause as we flipped over several times, finally landing upside down on our roof. I was engulfed in white light as I crawled out of the car on broken glass. I could see my grandmother's bloodied body in a heap still inside the car. I screamed in terror for what seemed like an eternity. Finally, she awoke and climbed out of the car. The accident further triggered in me a persistent fear that Gram would die one day too, and I would be all alone.

All this sent me into a downward spiral of crime, addiction, and juvenile incarceration.

Desperation is never a gift when you are experiencing it. Not all desperation is good desperation. It's not something that should be an excuse to stay in an abusive situation. But desperation is a gift when it becomes a teacher, showing us who we really are and what we are capable of. It teaches us to more fully trust and rely upon God.

Perhaps it takes a fall from Eden to first encounter the G.O.D. who is always coming and calling out after us, "Where are you?" The good news is that God is with us in our desperation. That's the gift, that we are not alone.

God is waiting for us to turn and receive a healing embrace.

3

ADOPTION

For you did not receive a spirit of slavery to fall back into fear,
but you have received a spirit of adoption. When we cry, "Abba!
Father!"

Romans 8:15 NRSV

He came from a rural lower-class peasant family. He didn't know much about his biological origins, as he was adopted into the royal house as an infant. All he had known was the bustle of the city, a hub of culture, education, and power. People moved fast here. It seemed as if new, behemoth structures were erected almost daily. He was surrounded by excitement, luxury, and power.

Most of the economy and construction was built on the backs of a slave labor force, but that didn't bother him all that much. The current scenario provided a comfortable life for him. All over the world, children died of starvation and sickness. Many people lived in grinding poverty. In his house, as a member of the royal family, he had access to the best education, the finest food, and the royal physicians and scientists. He was adopted into the most elite ruling family in the world. No nation came close to their economic, religious, and military dominance.

Now and again, he would watch the slave crews making their mud bricks, carrying stones and water, and erecting the country's great monolithic forms with an ingenious system of ropes, pulleys, and lifts. The people groaning underneath the weight of those tasks were biologically his ancestors, the Hebrews. It was from this slave population that he was adopted into the king's house. His name,

מֹשֶׁה (mo-sheh), meant "drawing out (from the water)." It was a name given to him by his adoptive mother, a daughter of the king. The story she always told him was that he simply washed up on the shore, and into her care ever since. The gods had sent him to her, and she was grateful. Moses was grateful too . . . for a time.

For some reason, something was different inside him that day. A taskmaster, being particularly brutal with one of the slaves, beat the fragile man senseless for no apparent reason. The stirrings of compassion in Moses' heart led to an intense anger, and before he knew it, he had a stone in his hand. He looked both ways, making sure no one could see, and then, in a cold and out-of-character act, he struck the taskmaster repeatedly. He just snapped and didn't finish striking until the man lay lifeless in a pool of blood. He dragged the man's body to a nearby construction lot and buried him in the sand.

Days later, the murder was on the front page of the *Egyptian Times*, and chatter circulated among the slave workforces. Word on the street was that Moses, "he who was drawn from the water," had committed cold-blooded murder.

When Pharoah, his adoptive grandfather, discovered his crime, justice came swiftly. Not only did he reject Moses, but he ordered his execution. With no other options, Moses fled into the desert (Exod 2:15). Instantly, he changed from an elite member of the royal family to a fleeing fugitive whose only purpose was to survive in a hostile terrain. In the desert, Moses would become familiar with the gift of desperation.

Yet it was in his place of desolation that Moses found himself. While in hiding from Egyptian justice, Moses got married, made a life, and found a renewed sense of purpose. Life seemed to be going well, all things considered. He grew older.

Then came that fateful day when he encountered a strange new god speaking to him out of a flaming bush. This wasn't just any god, though: it was YHWH, the God of his biological parents, the God of his ancestors. In that moment, his sense of purpose grew, and he discovered he was part of a larger story, one that revealed a part of himself that he had long forgotten. This obscure God, who identified himself simply as "I Am," was requiring Moses to go back and demand the release of his oppressed people.

Moses would have to return to the place of his adoption, his Garden of Eden, the onetime refuge that had become a living hell overnight. He would have to return and face the very people who had taken him in and given him shelter, but now as an opponent demanding justice and freedom for the ones they had enslaved and exploited for centuries.

His new challenge was going to ask a lot of him. It would require him to make an upward movement toward a God he didn't know very well, an inward movement toward an inner self he didn't know very well, and an outer movement toward others that would involve risking his own life. He was entirely vulnerable in every way.

Additionally, he was not qualified for the job. Not only did he have a speech impediment, which would diminish his ability to tell the king to "let my people go," but he had questions in his own soul about who his "people" even were. Besides, he was a murderer and a fugitive of the greatest nation on earth. Was he just to march back in and make demands? He was the worst man for the job. This strange God named YHWH couldn't have chosen a more unfit messenger.

Moses embarked on a journey of vulnerability. He would have to draw upon deep inner resources he didn't know he had and to trust and rely on a God who had placed a calling on his life, a vocation to be a liberator.

As the story played out, Moses, "drawn from the water," led his people through a split sea. They were "drawn from the water" into a new liberation. Through Moses' leadership, they made that long journey together. The central story of the Old Testament is inextricably bound with the life of this one man. We know that it was through facing his own inner woundedness that he became a wounded healer. Moses took the deep brokenness of his circumstances and led others to a place of liberation. He painted with ashes, and because of his journey, entire tribes, nations, and peoples consider him their spiritual ancestor and patriarch.

One of those descendants was Itzchak Belter, whose story was told in chapter 1. As a seven-year-old boy, he was "adopted" into Janusz Korczak's Warsaw orphanage, a place he would later describe as his personal "Garden of Eden." In comparison to the circumstances of his home life, the orphanage was a place of refuge and hope. A place where a stranger, affirmed, nurtured, and loved him into being. The experience of abandonment or forced disconnection from biological parents is a wound that never heals. Yet, it is that very desperation that sets up a child for the gracious wonders of adoption.

There is something powerfully redemptive about adoption. A person with no family is provided a new family. Adoption is the language that the apostle Paul would employ to describe the experience of becoming a follower of Jesus. (Rom 8:15). The Spirit of adoption can transform us from fearful slaves to God's joyful "children." It is this language that is used to describe the experience of coming into the church (Eph 1:4–5 NRSV). Jesus warned his disciples that following him would cause division in families (Luke 12:52–53). But he also made it clear that belonging to the community of faith superseded even biological familial bonds (Matt 12:46-50). The church is a big, messy blended family where everyone is adopted.

Moses experienced a spirit of joy through his adoption into the royal family of Egypt, but simultaneously a spirit of slavery. He didn't find true freedom and sonship until he made the inner journey to find himself and then joined himself with that community of vulnerable and imprisoned slaves. He found true life in downward mobility.

＊＊＊＊＊

Some of us have to lose our freedom to find it. It took me lying on the floor of a jail cell in ultimate confinement to find true freedom for the first time in my life. I too was able to recall an Edenic place, my own orphanage of sorts. I was able to remember my adoption.

After Grandpa's death, Gram took me back up to Elmira to visit my aunt and cousins. Gram was the one who first taught me how to paint with ashes. In some way she was forcing me to face my fears and embrace the pain, so I could find healing. She took me to the National Soaring Museum, where we looked at all the motorless flight exhibits. The high point of the day was being towed up in a sail plane, where the pilot let me take the stick.

I looked down on those same mountains that had been like a prison for me. I imagined I could see the spot where my stepfather had left me to die. Now I was flying high above all that. I had survived and could accomplish anything. I smiled, I cried, and I soared. It was a painting-with-ashes moment.

My grandparents had legally adopted me. They had taken me to church regularly those first ten years of my life. Leading up to his death, my grandfather had attended sporadically, but my grandma never missed. In my earliest memories, I am sitting beside her, front pew on the preacher's right, at St. Mark's United Methodist Church in Ocala, Florida. I am standing with those precious folks as we sing our faith together.

Shortly after my mother abandoned me, Pastor Holland Vaughn and the people of St. Mark's gathered around me at my infant baptism. Together they took responsibility to surround me with "a community of love and forgiveness" and to raise me in the family of God. They stepped into the gap of loss and abandonment in my life. They fed me through their never-ending potlucks and loved me into a relationship with Jesus. By being adopted by my grandparents, I was also being adopted by them. *Ubuntu*. I am, because they are.

My experience of church was of a healing community that was accessible, safe, and real.

We looked at those three terms before. But let's revisit them again:

1. *Accessible*: My church was close, in my neighborhood, and spoke a common language I could understand, just as Jesus did when he came and made his dwelling among us (John 1:14).

2. *Safe*: It was a place of healing, not harm, an environment of grace, an inclusive space where all were welcome and where the "good news" was made available to all (Luke 4:18–19).

3. *Real*: The pastor and the people were honest about their real wounds. They processed their pain in uncensored language, with prayer that brought real healing (James 5:16).

When Grandpa died, Reverend Vaughn took me under his wing. He drove me around to pastor meetings in his old green Oldsmobile. On one occasion, he looked into my eyes and said, "Michael, you are going to be a pastor one day." I found his pronouncement humorous, first, because I had no intention of ever becoming a pastor, and second, because in that season, I was starting to run with neighborhood gangs and engage in unholy activities.

Pastor Vaughn made me the acolyte, the person who would light the altar candles and put them out to begin and conclude the worship service. He told me I had the most important job in the service, to "bring the flame of God into the house of God and to carry it out into the world." As the acolyte, week after week I carried my candle lighter and sat beside him at the altar. I watched the people laugh, cry, fall asleep, and occasionally shout an enthusiastic "Amen!" From the "preacher's bench" behind the pulpit, I observed this master bring the Bible to life. Subconsciously I was reasoning through my own theology, experiencing God's love through God's people, and absorbing the Word through the biblical sermons, the creeds, and the hymns as we sang our faith together.

I went to Sunday school, and even the youth group for a while, mostly because of the girls. I remember being happy I was a Methodist because at the church across the street, the girls had to wear dresses to their ankles, long-sleeve shirts, and they weren't allowed to dance. Not us Methodists! We danced, had lock-ins, made out, and then sang songs about Jesus. It was great.

In those first years immediately following my grandfather's death, I was living a kind of double life. I was still connected to the church, spending time with Pastor Vaughn, serving as the acolyte, trying to be a good Christian boy, if you will. But simultaneously I was also starting to explore another world.

When my grandfather first became sick, Grandma would drop me off at the local skating rink so she could be with him at the hospital. I was a natural skater. I played roller hockey and joined the speed team. Our team in Ocala was led by coach Renee Hildebrand, an internationally known inline speed coach who has trained several athletes who crossed over to Olympic ice skating.

On the speed team I found a tribe whom I felt connected to. It was a culture of young athletes. We took training seriously and competed at regional and national meets. Speed skating gave my life a focus and helped me get out of my head. When I was skating, I wasn't thinking about all the dysfunction in my family or my grandfather's illness. I was able to win some of the competitions in my age group.

The skating rink also had another dimension. It was essentially a kind of nightclub for horny teenagers. Yeah, church girls liked to make out, but these girls were going all the way. As we were not yet adults, going to nightclubs, dancing, drinking, and those kinds of activities were off the table. But at the skating rink we had our own version of those activities. There was a dance floor, but there was also the skating rink floor itself. Jam skating, shuffle skating, and couples skating were primary activities of every session.

The speed team consisted of the elite "rink rats." We were the cool kids that others emulated and wanted to hang out with. We didn't have to pay to get into general skate sessions, we received free drinks and snacks at the concession stand, and we helped the floor guards set up and conduct games and races.

There was also a kind of never-ending soap opera of hookups and breakups. It seemed that every week there was some new drama to follow. So-and-so was now going out with so-and-so, or some supercouple had broken up. The never-ending drama was often expressed in the apex of the couples skate. This is when a couple would take to the floor, hand and hand, and skate to romantic '90s R&B hits. Rink rats would line the walls to watch who was coupled up with whom. Occasionally this whirlwind of hookups and breakups would end in fistfights.

The "all night skate" was the Sin City weekend of skating-rink life. This was the opportunity for making out and sexual exploration.

Couples would hide out around the rink walls or under blankets on the floor to experiment. My first encounters with French kissing, spooning, fondling, and oral sex happened in the skating rink. The rumor mill would often get fired up over who had hooked up with whom. A string of these kinds of interactions led me to my first sexual encounter at twelve years old.

I was deeply in love with a blonde-haired, blue-eyed beauty. She was a newcomer to the skating-rink scene. I dumped a string of ongoing relationships to be with her. I remember building up the courage to ask her on our first couples skate. She said yes! Our relationship progressed, and one night she invited me to sneak over to her house. I skated four and a half miles one way to sneak into her window. Shortly after I entered her room, her father started banging on the door, which forced me to flee out the window in only my underwear, skates in hand. Her dad came charging out of the house. I watched him pacing up and down the road, yelling after me from the safety of a nearby playground. Then, I put on my skates and skated home wearing only a pair of tighty-whities.

Shortly afterward, she broke up with me. This did not look good on a skating rink player's résumé. Somehow in my twelve-year-old mind I had us being married and living happily ever after. I was head over heels "in love." While none of this deterred the local rink girls from pursuing me, I was devastated. This was another blow to my self-worth, and it fueled a vicious cycle of sex addiction sometimes referred to as M.A.P: masturbation, adultery, and pornography. It would continue throughout most of my young life.

The neighborhood boys and I had started stealing pornographic magazines, cigarettes, and beer from a local convenience store. Looking at the magazines together in our clubhouse led to experimentation and group masturbation. One of the older boys loosely connected to our group, invited me over and manipulated me into a sexual situation. When I tried to put a stop to it, he sexually abused me. This was another incident that sent me into deep shame. While I did have some homosexual experimentation with my friends, I was sexually attracted solely to the opposite sex. These incidents together drove me to seek out more and more sexual relationships with a string of girls. If I could get them to have sex with me, it fed my self-worth, at least for a brief period.

These developments caused me to lose connection with the church. I felt like a hypocrite. I had made out with some of the church girls in my youth group, but whenever I tried to move past that, they would shut me down. So, I decided they were a waste of time. I knew all of this was wrong, but I was becoming full of resentment, fear, and shame.

In addition to roller hockey, I played many other sports, mostly to get away from inhabiting my own head. This included several seasons of baseball, becoming a certified lifeguard at the city pool and swim meets, basketball, and sandlot football. I grew more and more serious about competitive inline speed skating. I traveled around the US for meets. I had envisioned myself becoming an Olympic skater. All that changed for me when I entered high school.

My mother had moved back to the Ocala area, and she would drop by every now and again. But she was addicted to crack, and her addiction had progressed to the point that she became a streetwalking prostitute. I remember driving down South Pine, the major strip of addiction and vice in our town, and seeing my mother out on the street. One night, I approached a car in my front yard to find my mother giving oral sex to a dealer for crack. I banged on the window in anger, but she waved me away and went back to the task. She was in and out of jail, and every time she was released, she would come crash with grandma and me, promising she was going to get clean. It was only a matter of time before she took off again.

My mom provided me with my first pornographic videos. These were VHS tapes, the main video technology of the day. Video pornography was a whole different world from magazines. I would spend much of my young life in that world. On some of the occasions when she lived with us, my mom would come into my bedroom and give me strange massages. I was sexually aroused by this. More heaping coals of shame poured down on my head, along with shame's evil twin: guilt.

Each time mom came home, she had a new King James Version Gideons Bible. She would write notes in the margins. When she left, she would always leave her Bible behind, but I would read those notes, trying to understand her and what she was thinking. My little brother, McKinley, lived off and on between us and his paternal grandmother. His life was even harder than mine. Once when Mom lived with us, she stole a bunch of my clothes and my bike to trade them for drugs, then disappeared. What had started as confusion about my mom was quickly turning into hatred toward her.

In my ninth-grade history class, the teacher showed one of those "say no to drugs" videos that were mandatory for schools during the crack epidemic of the 1980s and 1990s. It was an anonymous documentary about a female crack addict and prostitute named "Kris." Kris talked about her experiences on the streets and shared stories about the times she was raped and how she had lost her children and her dignity. The woman in the video was my mother. She had cut a deal with the sheriff's department to make the video in exchange for getting out of jail time. Some of my classmates who knew me well recognized her as my mother. I could feel my peers' eyes on me in that class.

I left school that day and never went back. I decided from that day forward that I would rather carve out a life for myself by any means necessary than go back and deal with that kind of humiliation. My key financial model would be the sale of narcotics. I had been sleeping with a girl who had moved in two houses down and now descended deeper into sex addiction. I also immersed myself in alcohol and drugs.

My neighborhood friends and I dove deeply into the world of Dungeons & Dragons. I became a voracious reader of novels, D&D materials, and religious texts from many religions. I created a fictional RPG (role-playing game) world through dozens of handwritten journals and drew out maps of the various lands. I spent countless hours writing a series of novels that I hoped to one day publish as my magnum opus. As Dungeon Master, I led my childhood friends through campaigns in unknown worlds of our imagination. A bunch of high school dropouts, we essentially educated ourselves through D&D. After I had run away several times, my grandmother decided it was better to tolerate this behavior than lose me entirely to the streets.

One day, my mother came back from her latest incarceration and brought a peace offering. A group of my friends and I gathered in the bungalow in my grandparents' backyard, where we now played D&D night and day. There, in the same place I had first felt hatred toward my little brother in his crib, I snorted cocaine for the first time with my mother. We stayed up all night doing lines, smoking cigarettes, playing cards, and talking crazy. I remember one of the older guys that hung with our group saying to mom, "That's your son. He's just a kid. Don't you think this is kind of fucked up?"

Before the night was over, we ran out of cocaine. Mom and I decided I could trade a gold chain that one of my girlfriends had bought me for more coke, so we did that. The party continued into the next day. It was through my mom that I was able to get connected with some high-level drug dealers. What followed was a tragic series of events that included juvenile detention facilities, residential programs for youthful offenders, and finally jail.

The catch in adoption into God's family is that we have a choice to accept or reject it.

We can embrace the invitation to be children of God's family, or we can refuse it. God never forces us to receive grace. He lets us make that decision for ourselves. But for those of us who choose to run away from God, we learn that God never gives up pursuit. Even when we create a life for ourselves that can become a hell on earth, the God we encounter in Jesus is one who "descended into hell" to find us.[1]

My experience of a healing community that was accessible, safe, and real would ultimately change the trajectory of my life. Those days were a crucial season in my formation: I could turn fully toward the nurturing of Pastor Vaughn and the community that called me their beloved child. Or I could take the trip with the friends in my neighborhood down a road that would lead me far away from home.

The allure of darkness proved to be too much. I left my spiritual orphanage behind and burned the adoption papers.

4

HURT PEOPLE HURT PEOPLE

Then Paul said: "I am a Jew, born in Tarsus of Cilicia, but brought
up in this city. I studied under Gamaliel and was thoroughly
trained in the law of our ancestors. I was just as zealous for God
as any of you are today. I persecuted the followers of this Way
to their death, arresting both men and women and throwing
them into prison, as the high priest and all the Council can
themselves testify. I even obtained letters from them to their
associates in Damascus and went there to bring these people
as prisoners to Jerusalem to be punished."

Acts 22:2–5

After graduation, Itzchak Belfer returned as a volunteer to the orphanage where he was raised, to help the younger children. When
the Nazi forces conquered Poland, he and a friend decided to go
join the Soviets to fight against the Nazis. In 1939 Belfer said his
final goodbye to Janusz Korczak, his caretaker during his years in the
Warsaw orphanage.

At the same time Korczak and his orphans were being marched
singing and holding hands from the Warsaw orphanage to the Treblinka extermination camp, a ten-old-year Dutch boy born in Ni-
jkerk, Netherlands, was considering study at the minor seminary.
The oldest of four children, he loved to dress up as a priest, conducting mass for his three siblings, who served as his first congregation.

That boy was Henri J. Nouwen, the son of Laurent J. M. Nouwen, a tax lawyer, and Maria Nouwen, who worked as a bookkeeper

for her family's business in Amersfoort. Laurent had overcome a childhood of poverty to lift his family into the upper class. He was self-made and driven, and he encouraged his children to strive for success. Maria was devoutly religious and maternal, and she encouraged her children toward spirituality in the Catholic tradition. Young Henri Nouwen grew up in the shadow of World War II. But his woundedness flowed from a different source than poverty and abandonment.

People sometimes make judgments on the severity of someone's circumstances. Particularly when the pain is our own, it can feel worse than someone else's. Yet, every person is wounded, and to every individual those wounds are just as powerful and real as the next person's. Jesus challenges our proclivity to grade people's brokenness. We love to point out the speck in another's eye while a plank protrudes from our own (Matt 7:3). A central point of Jesus' message highlights how our actions flow from what is in our hearts (12:34). Sinful actions that harm others are the outward expression of wounds that go untreated.

One of the greatest challenges of Jesus' message is this: even if we have entertained evil in our own mind, we have already sinned, because our inner condition remains fragmented (Matt 5:21–28). This means the playing field is completely leveled. All people stand equally in need of God's grace.

While all wounds are not created equal, we are all equally wounded. We are all in need of healing.

From his earliest recollections, Henri Nouwen experienced a profound sense of uncertainty and shame. He was obsessed as a child with asking his parents if they loved him. He felt a deep and seemingly unquenchable longing to be loved. Because his father was an independent and success-oriented person who expected his children to be the same, Henri never felt that his father loved him unconditionally. Henri's siblings have questioned if this was merely Henri's perspective, nevertheless, Henri carried a wound of isolation and a need to be loved throughout his life, which was aggravated by the fact that he was homosexual.[1] Paradoxically, it was Henri's wounded-ness that helped him become increasingly vulnerable and open in his own teaching and writing, which brought healing to millions.

Henri's uncle Toon Ramselaar was a Roman Catholic priest in the Archdiocese of Utrecht and a cofounder of the Service Inter-national de Documentation Judéo-Chrétienne. The young Henri looked up to his uncle and, yearning for his mother's total approval, he committed to become a priest. In his studies, Nouwen became particularly fascinated with the field of psychology. He was able to bridge those two fields in a way that was unique, and as a Catholic priest, he introduced a whole new language and conversation around spirituality.

It was psychologist Carl Jung who first used the metaphor of a wounded healer to describe one dimension of the therapist-patient relationship. He drew from the Greek myth of Asclepius. In one version of this myth, Asclepius is raised by his teacher and surrogate father, Chiron. Chiron was famous for his healing powers. He in-structed people in the arts of healing and music but ironically him-self suffered from a wound that would never heal.[2]

Nouwen draws upon this imagery in his seminal work, *The Wounded Healer: Ministry in Contemporary Society*. He begins by diagnosing the postmodern context, particularly the erosion of the myth of progress. While science and technology have been used as a force for massive good, they also paradoxically have created the plight of "nuclear man." The same technological advancements that have created material progress can be used to destroy the planet. Nouwen grew up in the age that witnessed the creation and deployment of the first atomic bombs.

Nouwen describes his age as one of historic discontinuity, in which an entire generation broke with the values of the previous generation. In this "fragmented ideology," the misplaced hope in the myth of progress has been lost. The church, which once provided the legitimating narrative for Western society, lost its relevance and authority. Now in the cracks of a pluralistic and fragmented world, ministers once respected are left shivering in the shadows of irrel-evancy and impotency.

These inconsistencies were aggravated by the minster's realization that she or he is just as wounded as the people placed in her or his care. Because of this, Nouwen noted, ministers struggle with a sense of identity, and many default to professionalism, hiding behind the armor of training and education, which further diminishes their ability to be present with the wounded ones seeking help. Nouwen argues that presence, vulnerability, and hospitality are the way to be with the wounded. It is the cracks that let the light in. By sharing together in the universal condition of woundedness, we allow the true healer to touch our wounds. This requires not professionalism, but vulnerability.

Earlier I referenced Nouwen's framework of the spiritual journey as three prayerful movements toward wholeness: toward our truest self "inward," toward God "upward," and toward each other "outward." These three movements help hurt people move toward becoming wounded healers.

These three movements are inextricably linked. A movement toward our inner self is a movement toward God, for there in the solitude, we discover God. The move toward our other is a move toward finding God in our other, recognizing God was already there before we got there. These movements are not a one-way street, but a constant back-and-forth. A wounded healer's journey is never complete in this world. We are in a continual movement of healing that includes this matrix of relationships.

<hr/>

Some say that behind every serial killer, despot, or rapist is a wounded upbringing. This is partly true. When we human beings become wounded in the movement between ourselves, others, and God, we can become hurt people who hurt people.

Dallas Willard describes the effects of a deficit within the social dimension of our humanity: "The infant who is not received in love by a mother and others is wounded for life and may even die. It must bond with its mother or someone in order to take on a self and a life.

And rejection, no matter how old one is, is a sword thrust to the soul that has literally killed many."[3]

How can several hurt people, living at the same time, and bearing similar wounds, respond to them so differently? Consider Charles Manson, who was born on November 12, 1934, to a sixteen-year-old mother, his biological father unknown. Manson was born just three years before Desmond Tutu, and two years after Nouwen. The same year a little girl named Maya Angelou would be raped by her mother's boyfriend in St. Louis, Missouri. Manson was born when a little orphan named Itzchak Belfer was at Korczak's "Garden of Eden."

Manson's stepfather was an abusive alcoholic, and his mother went to prison when he was a young boy. He launched into a life of criminality. He reportedly set his school on fire when he was nine. Eventually he became the cult leader of the "Manson Family," a commune based in California. His followers were responsible for a series of nine murders at four locations.

Each of these individuals—Manson, Tutu, Angelou, Belfer, Nouwen and Korczak—experienced great adversity, in profoundly different ways. Each of them was wounded. Yet, the same wounds that drove Manson to become a cult leader and murderer, drove others to become priests, poets, artists, authors, spiritual leaders, and healers. How is this possible? What makes the difference?

While some wounded people wound people, others find a way to use their wounds to heal others.

Hurt people hurt people, but healed people heal people.

When we are trapped in our own agony of isolation, fear, and resentment, we act out from our brokenness and bring harm to others. Alcoholics and drug addicts typically use substances in some attempt to self-medicate harm that was done to them. Ironically, in the process of medicating our own wounds, we become unable to be present for others around us. Obsession with wounds inflicted upon us leads us to wound others.

Healing begins when we come to terms with our wounds, embrace them, confess them, make amends for the harms we've caused, and dedicate ourselves to healing others with the same affliction. This journey facilitates the same kind of radical turning in the other direction that we see in Paul the apostle. Paul went from executing Christians to being executed as one. He transformed from a wounded harmer to a wounded healer. He had all the credentials to become the ultimate religious zealot, but through an encounter with Christ, embraced a journey of downward mobility toward solidarity with the ones he had formerly oppressed.

I was a hurt person hurting people. I was thirteen when I was incarcerated for the first time. I had been arrested multiple times before but had been bonded out or released to await a court date. On this particular occasion, I was the passenger in a car accident. My friend was driving me to sell a large quantity of marijuana, and someone randomly rear-ended us at a stoplight.

When the police arrived with a K9 unit, we knew one of us was going to jail. I took responsibility for the marijuana, so that one of us was me. My first night in the juvenile detention center, I knew I was in a different world. I was stripped naked alongside a group of other boys, and we were made to bend over and cough so the guards could examine our anal cavities. Next, we were doused with lice powder and washed down in a shower room. We were given underwear and colored jumpsuits based on the level of our offense: red, blue, or orange.

The facility was so crowded that children and teenagers slept in "boats" on the floor. These were essentially pallets that could hold a mat, blanket, and pillow. I remember being grateful my first time that I slept in a boat in the hallway rather than locked in a room with strangers.

That first morning I was sitting in the recreation room for the morning roll call. A trio of regulars was sitting behind me, breathing down my neck. One of the boys, whose nickname was Stone, told me, "I like those shoes." Everything I had heard from my friends who had been locked up was that you had to show strength or people would take advantage of you. I said, "Well, be ready to fight me for them, then."

The boys sitting with Stone started getting riled up and shaming Stone for letting me talk to him that way.

After roll call, we went back into the hallway and Stone and his buddies followed me in. I turned around and had my first juvenile detention fistfight. Stone and I began fighting, and then one of his friends, whose nickname was Cockeye, jumped in and started punching me. It felt like we fought forever. All of the other boys whooped and hollered. The guards finally responded and slammed us all to the ground.

I had participated in my share of fistfights before that day, but I was by no means an experienced fighter. There were daily altercations all over the facility. Some of the guards even set up different inmates to fight and placed bets on who would win. Now I knew why they called JDC "gladiator camp." Children entered that place and either were victimized, abused, and raped by other inmates, or came out a hardened criminal. Those were the two main options. Juvenile detention facilities, jails, and prisons are communities where hurt people hurt people.

Some teenagers seemed to make a home in the juvenile facility. They started their lifelong journey of institutionalization there. I was never comfortable with incarcerated life. I never accepted it as "home." However, that wasn't enough to deter me from continuing to commit crimes.

After I got out, my buddies and I turned a normal lower-class neighborhood on the edge of the projects into a hotbed of crime and drug dealing. Many of us on Northeast Ninth Avenue in Ocala had lost one or both parents to the crack epidemic. At least a dozen of my friends had come from broken homes. Mom or Dad was missing in action, incarcerated, or strung out.

My best friends were two brothers, D and J, who lived three houses down. The three of us were raised by our grandmothers. Our little gang of juvenile dropouts/felons moved from playing D&D to committing petty crimes: stealing, breaking and entering, and the like. This moved quickly to assault, sales and possession of narcotics, and carrying firearms.

By the time I was sixteen, I was a full-blown alcoholic and ac-complished drug dealer. I would buy large quantities of cocaine, marijuana, LSD, and Ecstasy (MDMA), for the purposes of sales and a bit of recreational use. I had a "triple beam" in my bedroom, along with containers full of baggies and all the necessary paraphernalia for distribution. I would cut the product, weigh it, and bag it for my col-leagues to distribute from one of the three trap houses on our street.

I did all of this at first from my grandmother's home. She ini-tially fought me, begged, and pleaded for me to stop. I laid out two options for her: she could quit resisting and let me do my thing, or I would leave. While not explicitly giving formal permission, she al-lowed the former.

Gram and I had a classic codependent relationship. Her fear of being alone and releasing me fully to the streets led her to pseudo-authorize my downward spiral of criminality. We clung to a toxic de-pendency on each other. Sometimes there would be customers lined up from my bedroom, down the hall, and into the living room. My grandmother sat in the living room in her old pink chair, where she would smoke cigarettes and read her Upper Room daily devotional and the Bible. As people waited to get back in my room to get their fix, Grandma would strike up conversations about Jesus. She would talk to my customers about their lives and let them know she was praying for them. Through this activity, my grandmother earned the hood name "Grams" to a whole generation of street kids. She became a kind of mother to many of my friends who didn't have any parents. They loved her and would protect her even to the point of violence.

In time, my childhood entrepreneurial skills kicked in and my method for distributing drugs grew more complex. I would load up each of my friends with "bonus packs," so every batch they sold had an internal profit mechanism built in. They would bring back the money, and I would give them another bundle of prepackaged prod-uct. I personally dealt with the clientele who bought in bulk. This included lawyers, doctors, business owners, and community leaders.

By the time I was seventeen, I had purchased my own vehicles and home and blown lots of money on vacations across the state. I bought Grams a sky blue Cadillac Sedan de Ville, which she absolutely hated. She called it her "mobster car" and preferred her old beat-up Ford LTD Crown Victoria. While she completely detested my activities, I made sure that she never lacked for anything.

As a teenager, I started setting up legitimate limited-liability companies as cover-ups for the illegal activity. This gave me space to learn how to run businesses. I started dreaming about going fully legit one day.

In the early '90s, lowriders were a thing, cars with special rims that made them sit low to the ground. Tinted windows. Big stereo systems for lots of bass. Tupac and Biggie dominated the gangsta rap scene, and pop culture emulated the "thug life."

Our normal mode was to hang out on different street corners, bumping music from the fifteen-inch speaker systems in our trunks, smoking weed, and drinking. We were notorious on the boulevard for pulling up in crowds of people, jumping out, and starting fights. We robbed people and stole women from our rivals. We did anything we wanted. This had made us many enemies. Several lowrider clubs and a few actual gangs had us in their crosshairs. We thought we were invincible.

One night, a pink Geo Tracker came rolling slowly down our street. We guarded this segment of Ninth Avenue as a no-go zone for our enemies. This pink Tracker belonged to one of our rivals, a gang that masqueraded as a lowrider club. Once we noticed them pass by, a group of about twenty of us went out into the road, talking smack, yelling profanities, trying to get them to stop. They quickly bolted off down the road just out of sight.

I was walking beside Johanna, my girlfriend at the time, when suddenly gunshots rang out. Our rivals fired into the crowd of us. I felt the heat of a bullet pass by my face, right between Johanna and me. In the world of street gangs, this was a declaration of war, and war was exactly what happened.

I often look back on that night and wonder about the probability of a bullet passing by my face so close that I could hear it like an angry wasp and feel its heat. If its trajectory had been altered by only inches one way or another, you would not be reading these words right now. It was a miracle that I wasn't hit.

Many of my friends growing up were not so fortunate. They died in gun battles, overdosed on drugs, or succumbed to AIDS and other STDs (another prominent feature of the '80s, '90s, and 2000s). Later, those streets claimed Johanna's life. Some have experienced an even worse fate: they have experienced institutionalization and have been incarcerated most of their lives.

For me, the close call that night indeed sparked a war. After multiple altercations with our rivals, some of which included an exchange of gunfire, one group decided to specifically target me for my role as the ringleader. On a late summer's eve of 1994, when I was fourteen, a handful of armed men pulled up in front of my grandmother's house and opened fire. The police reported that they fired approximately thirteen bullets into our home in less than one minute, then fled the scene.

The small home was lit up with bullets that passed through the front wall and landed in the back wall. Bullets passed through doors and windows. Fragments of home and furniture were sent flying into the air.

The problem for my rivals was that I wasn't actually home. My car was home, but I was riding with someone else, conducting an illegal transaction. My grandmother, however, was home. She was sitting at the kitchen table, doing a puzzle, something she often did; praying for me; and waiting up to see if I would come home alive.

A bullet passed through the back of her kitchen chair. The chairs were heavy wood, painted white, with slats that ran from the seat to the top arch. The bullet hit the slat, deflected down, and embedded in the table leg. The bullet was inches away from grandmother's back. The probability of this happening is one in a million. Again, a miracle.

After arriving home to swarms of police and detectives all over our home trying to discover what had happened, I was enraged. I was ready to call my band of brothers and seek revenge. The cops started questioning me about who, what, when, and where. None of their questions received any answers. Our street code was to die before we would snitch.

Emerging from the shadowy figures of investigators and forensic specialists in the swirling blue lights, a round man with an Indiana Jones hat and trench coat approached me.

"Michael, can we talk?" he asked.

"I don't know anything," I snapped back.

"My name is Pastor Dan. Your grandmother called me about what happened here tonight. I'm the pastor at St. Mark's," he said.

I had no idea how to respond.

Pastor Dan had been supporting my grandmother through all my insane and illegal activities. There was a group of folks at the church who prayed for me regularly. They were a safe community for my grandmother to share about the terror I had brought to her life.

"Michael, you know you need to stop this shit. Your grand-mother was almost killed tonight."

After a tongue-lashing, he said, "Do you mind if I pray for you?"

He took my hand and began praying. I didn't resist him. I don't remember what he said, but I did feel the strange sensation of being cared for by another man with no strings attached. He awakened in me what seemed like distant memories of my childhood faith.

"Why don't you come talk to me at the church sometime? Here's my card." Pastor Dan gave me his card, turned, and walked away.

It was a night of miraculous intervention. What would have happened if my grandmother's chair had been positioned inches an-other way? What kind of rage would I have embraced if the slat of that chair back hadn't changed the trajectory of that bullet by mere inches? What would have become of me without the interference of that ballsy, fedora-wearing, cursing, praying preacher?

It would not be the last time we would talk. His intervention was a significant moment in my journey from hurt person hurting people to becoming a wounded healer.

PART TWO:
SURRENDER

5

TO BE LOVED

We love because he first loved us.
1 John 4:19

The awkward, overweight child fled for his life, racing down the street as fast as his legs could move. Terror struck when he realized his attackers were gaining on him. "We're going to get you, Fat Freddy!" they taunted as they pursued the eight-year-old boy who had become the target of their bullying. Tears of anxiety and panic streamed down the boy's face. He was winded and couldn't run much longer. He prayed under his breath that he would make it to Mrs. Stewart's house, a widow and family friend who might save him from the assault.

By some miracle he made it onto her front porch. The bullies closed in as he banged on the door in sheer panic, praying that she was home. Mrs. Stewart opened the door and he fell into her sanctuary. His gang of assailants went on their way.

That shy little boy—"Fat Freddy," as his assailants called him—was Fred McFeely Rogers, better known to the world as Mister Rogers. He became an American television host, author, and producer. Until a recent surge in books and films about his life, it was widely unknown that he was also a Presbyterian minister. The world knows him as the creator and host of the preschool television series that ran from 1968 to 2001, *Mister Rogers' Neighborhood.*

For more than thirty years, Rogers subversively taught Christian values on a public television broadcasting network. He treated many issues with which wounded children were intimately familiar: divorce, disability, death, racism, anger, violence, education, war, and being kind in a hard world. Rogers received over forty honorary degrees, the Presidential Medal of Freedom, and a Lifetime Achievement Emmy, and was inducted into the Television Hall of Fame.

Rogers himself had experienced trauma as a child. He tended toward introversion and shyness and was also overweight. He struggled with bouts of asthma that left him frequently homebound. Because of his weight, he became the target of school bullies. He dreaded going to school. He had to be driven back and forth so they could not physically abuse him.[1]

In the midst of his shyness and a lonely childhood, Rogers found his superpower: imagination. He learned to play the piano at five, loved music, and started turning stuffed animals and puppets into ventriloquist dummies. The first episodes of his show happened in the studio of his bedroom, where he created a new world with his imagination. He painted with ashes by sharing that gift with the world, becoming a kind of modern saint for children. His childhood wounds became the source of healing to many.

In the film portraying his life, *A Beautiful Day in the Neighborhood*, Rogers is played by his distant cousin Tom Hanks. In one scene, he sits in a restaurant with Lloyd, a troubled friend who describes himself as "broken." Rogers responds, "I don't think you're broken." He then invites Lloyd to participate in an exercise there in the crowded restaurant. "We'll just take a minute and think about all of the people who loved us into being," he said.

As I watched, I began to reflect on all the people who had loved me into being. They surrounded me in a circle of love. I could see each one of their faces. Sitting in the theater, trying to hold back tears, I found myself wondering why such a simple exercise could make me weep. Then, in the silence, I heard sniffling and sobbing throughout the packed-out theater. A crowd of adults were weeping in concert together.

It was a powerful moment in the film and something I've tried to make a practice of in my own life. When I feel stressed or overwhelmed, I pause and prayerfully reflect on all the people who loved me into being.

We are only as broken as we see ourselves.

Is it possible that broken people can be loved into wholeness again? Fred Rogers believed it is.

One of Rogers' most important influences was Henri Nouwen. Rogers called him "one of my revered people in this life; he's a hero."[2] It was Nouwen's theology of vulnerability that impressed Rogers. Nouwen had chosen a path of downward mobility and left a life of academic prestige to live at the L'Arche community, where his daily responsibility was to care for a severely disabled man named Adam. He had to bathe, shave, dress, and feed Adam every day. Nouwen called Adam his teacher. Rogers was greatly impressed with this, and it informed his own inward, outward, and upward spiritual journey.

What Fred Rogers taught us most was that we are special and worthy of love. Every person longs to be loved. Love can turn a hurt person who hurts people into a wounded healer.

What's the difference between a Charles Manson and a Maya Angelou? Both experienced similar traumas in their childhood. Both carried wounds that never healed. But Maya had her grandmother Annie, whom she called "Momma." Manson had no one. Maya was loved by at least one person in the formative years of her life. By all accounts Manson was not. Sometimes the trajectory of our wound-edness comes down to one thing: being loved by at least one other person. Research on resilience supports this claim.[3]

Award-winning children's author and Jesus follower Madeleine L'Engle said, "[If] your name isn't known, then it's a very lonely feeling." To be loved is to be named, to be known. In L'Engle's book *A Wind in the Door*, Meg asks the "singular cherubim" how someone is named. "Love," responds the angel. "That's what makes persons know who they are."[4]

In the early years of my life, there was a single person who loved me unconditionally: my grandmother, Marion Jean Beck. Despite all the codependency and our awkward partnership between drug dealer and living-room evangelist, my grandmother loved me in the best way she knew how.

Like all humans, she had strange idiosyncrasies. She smoked two packs of cigarettes a day as she read her Bible. She wasn't a person who expressed intimacy through touch but tried to show her love through her provision by meeting my physical needs. I cannot remember her ever saying, "I love you," but I knew that she did. She would pray before a meal, and then in the next breath say, "What the hell is wrong with you?" or call me a "little bastard" (and often appropriately so). She attended church every Sunday and always tried to drag me along.

Yet, the one way my grandmother expressed her love every day was in praying for me. No matter how deep into the darkness I went, she never gave up hope for me. She lifted me before God daily.

While I knew that my grandmother loved me, from the time my grandfather died, I intentionally disconnected from her. His death brought me face-to-face with the reality that Grandma would die too, and I would be all alone. While on the outside I projected an image of strength, underneath I was a scared little boy. I lived in the constant fear of her inevitable death. To avoid vulnerability, I was shielding my heart from that inevitable moment.

I was launched out into the world with few positive tools for successful living. In my teenage years, I ran far from the love of God and God's people. I spent my life as a very compartmentalized person, dividing myself and storing different personalities in different compartments. I felt lost, as if I were part of a huge production where all the players but me knew their parts. When I figured out which scene in the play we were in, I could put on the mask and play the part. But the curtain seemed to be ever closing.

I became a chameleon who could disguise myself and become a part of any scene, because inside I had no real identity. In the drug-ridden ghettos of Ocala, Florida, I created an identity that was strong enough to survive. The person that emerged was not the real me, but only a parody of my true self.

Author and healer Brennan Manning described the tendency of all human beings to create a "false self" who "buys into outside experiences to furnish a personal source of meaning."[5] He identified this false self as "the impostor." He goes on to say, "The impostor lives in fear . . . Impostors are preoccupied with acceptance and approval . . . The pursuit of money, power, glamour, sexual prowess, recognition, and status enhances one's self-importance and creates the illusion of success. The impostor is what he *does*."[6]

I have been "the impostor" most of my life. I always felt like an outsider. I could see the kids in school doing the deal called life so freely, so gracefully, with such enthusiasm. I was always looking for something external that could rearrange me internally. I never really felt a part of anything until I met alcohol and drugs. In those substances I found a "liquid courage." All fear, anxiety, and inferiority were washed down with a couple of swallows. Now I had found the spotlight; now I had found my place. I was full! Under the influence of substances, I could let Clark Kent go take a nap and bring out Superman. It took me a long time to discover that the very thing that made me feel like I had an *S* on my chest was actually my kryptonite.

I began to create this persona as early as twelve years old. The drug-dealing, gun-toting teenager, who had a gold grill in his mouth and "Thug 4 Life" tattooed on his arm was entirely an impostor, with a mask to hide my true self. I was like a stage actor. I created and played a role to survive my circumstances. Underneath it all, I was still the little ten-year-old boy who lost my grandpa . . . who was also my father. I lived with the unresolved dissonance of seeing him as a person I loved and turned to for shelter, and the horrible abuser that my mother and my aunt told me he was.

In some ways, I had to kill that little boy to survive.

That little boy did survive, though. I longed to be loved and to give love. In those days of darkness and death-dealing, somehow the birth of my daughter Caitlin awakened me to my true self. My sexual deviance had resulted in several pregnancies that ended in abortions. I became a teenage father at age fifteen. My oldest daughter, Ariel, while biologically not mine, was born from my heart. Although I "inherited" her through the relationship with my ex-wife, I have loved and raised her as my own. Genetics mean very little to me. She is as equally my daughter as her siblings, and I have been the only daddy she has known.

I wasn't present for Ariel's birth. I was eighteen when her sister, my first biological daughter Caitlin, was born. I can only describe the experience of her birth as the catalyst to a spiritual awakening. Of course, I was intoxicated and high in the delivery room. It was all quite confusing and traumatic. This little girl came kicking and screaming into the world as we all do. But when the nurse placed her in my arms, she suddenly got quiet and looked up into my eyes with a big goofy smile. I know they say newborns can't smile, but she did. As the nurse placed her in my arms, she said, "Here you go, Dad."

Those words penetrated and wrecked my frozen heart. It was as if time stood still for a moment. I felt the presence of what I know today to be the Holy Spirit. Tears welled up in my eyes. As I looked at that helpless little life, gazing up at me and relying on me for protection, care, and love, I realized the magnitude of my responsibility. I was "Dad" to a beautiful little baby named Caitlin Jean Beck now. She was counting on me to be that. I was the only one who could do the job.

I made a commitment in that moment to give C. J. the father I'd never had. She would not go through life the way I did, without a father or without parental love. I would protect her. I would love her.

One complication was that she was born in the height of my burgeoning drug empire. A group of self-identified homosexuals had moved onto Ninth Avenue. In those days, gay people were openly discriminated against and hated. Homophobia was at an all-time high. Throughout the '80s and '90s, the AIDS epidemic was ravaging the world. For a time, it was called the "gay plague." Gay men were perceived as making games of sexual conquest dangerous and even deadly. In street culture, all of this was amplified greatly.

"Faggots," "punks," and "bitches," as we called them, should be beaten, dealt with, and even killed. Now, a group of them had moved onto our block, just ten houses down from my drug-dealing outpost. On top of that, there were people in and out of their home from morning until night. As it turned out, they had their own quite complex and lucrative drug-dealing operation.

For a while, we declared open war on the "punks." Fistfights, altercations that included brandishing swords, and even drawing firearms on each other went on for months. It was a volatile and deadly situation. Some of our customers started going to them, and their customers started coming to us. The violent exchanges usually resulted in police showing up, jeopardizing both of our operations.

I could see that this was going to end badly for all of us. So, two of my closest associates and I, packing firearms, went down to the enemy headquarters. I asked to speak with their leader, Rick, and surprisingly he invited me in alone. Rick was stocky with a sandy blond curly mullet. He looked like an alligator wrestler fresh out of a swamp somewhere. He always wore several thick gold chains.

Basically, I laid it out for him that we had been safely dealing drugs on this street without bringing down major heat. Now, with our constant altercations, we were both in jeopardy of going to prison. We decided to form a peace pact. I would make my gang, the Ninth Avenue Boys, aware of this truce, and they would stop antagonizing Rick's people. He would do likewise. We celebrated this with a drink, and Rick invited me to talk to him anytime.

The Ninth Avenue Boys were not pleased with this arrangement. Some of them started to call me weak. But we could all agree it was good for business.

One day, Rick and a couple of his associates came down to my house. Their dealer had run dry, and their customers were jonesing. They needed to buy in bulk from me. Our truce over time became a business partnership. They were pumping out as much product if not more than we were. I was forced to confront my own homophobia and befriend whom I considered to be the enemy. I couldn't believe how quickly they moved large quantities of cocaine.

I began to form a deep and meaningful relationship with Rick. One weekend he invited me to see where all the magic happened. He took my ex-wife and me to an exclusively gay nightclub in Ocala. This place was "off the chain." People were having sex in the bathrooms and all kinds of crazy activity. Rick and his friends sat right at the bar and openly sold drugs to anybody who came in. It was as if their little club operated with immunity in regard to the law. In less than a half hour, we sold everything we had. Rick grinned. "I told you, you didn't bring enough." We went back and replenished the supply three more times, and each time we sold out in less than an hour.

Rick introduced me to the LGBTQ community and to another underworld beneath the underworld that I knew. High-profile people, law enforcement, politicians, and business owners were part of this secret community, and Rick introduced me to them.

Our partnership was really growing, and not only was the financial scenario positive for everyone, but Rick and I were becoming close friends. He befriended Gram, ate dinner with us, accompanied us on many vacations, and came to my children's birthday parties. We had built an illegal empire, and we were both buying new homes and vehicles and investing in legitimate businesses. At eighteen I had founded the company that I would run for the next decade. But Rick was a serious alcoholic. He drank to blackout every day and had a nasty habit of driving drunk.

One day, Rick, my two daughters, and I were watching a newly released movie called *The Prince of Egypt*, about the biblical Moses. He turned to me and said, "I know Grams believes—she is always trying to convert me—but do you believe in God?" I was emotionally moved by the film, and it was awakening all kinds of childhood memories.

"Yes. I do," I replied.

Rick smiled. "Yeah, me too. I pray every day. I know God doesn't want me doing what I do, but I don't know any other way."

"Same here." I smiled. "I do know I have to quit soon. I don't want to live in prison the rest of life. I want to be here for my daughters."

"Well, when you figure out how to do that, you let me know; we'll do it together." Rick laughed.

Two days later, I got a phone call just after midnight. Rick was dead. He'd been driving one of his new convertibles drunk with a group of friends when he ran into the back of a semitruck and was decapitated.

Some of my inner circle had been whispering that I was weak and spent too much time with the "faggots." One of my closest friends stole a large quantity of cocaine, and I had to respond with violence or lose all respect and street cred. Things were falling apart. When I decided to attend Rick's funeral, another one of my guys, responsible for security, said, "You're going to attend that punk's funeral? Not a good decision, boss."

Additionally, a couple of dirty cops with whom I had a complicated relationship sent me a message: "Stop now or get busted." I'd gotten connected with them when I was a kid, and they regularly used my mother to set up drug dealers. She would make buys while wearing a wire to get out of the jail time for her petty arrests. They were taking advantage of her, helping facilitate her destruction, and I kept their secret. But now they felt that I was getting too big for my britches. The writing was on the wall.

One night, I grabbed one of the Gideons Bibles that my mom had brought home from one of her stays at the Marion County Jail Hotel. I opened and stumbled upon Paul's letter to his protégé, Timothy. In 2 Timothy 1:5, Paul reminds this young leader that the faith that lived in his grandmother was now alive in him. I read Paul's words to Timothy—and it was as if God were speaking them directly to me:

> But mark this: There will be terrible times in the last days. People will be lovers of themselves, lovers of money, boastful, proud, abusive, disobedient to their parents, ungrateful, unholy, without love, unforgiving, slanderous, without self-control, brutal, not lovers of the good, treacherous, rash, conceited, lovers of pleasure rather than lovers of God—having a form of godliness but denying its power. Have nothing to do with such people. They are the kind who worm their way into homes and gain control over gullible women, who are loaded down with sins and are swayed by all kinds of evil desires, always learning but never able to come to a knowledge of the truth. (2 Tim 3:1–7)

As I read, I felt as if God was communicating directly to me, that this is who I had become. It was a perfect description of my life in that moment. Paul continues:

> But as for you, continue in what you have learned and have become convinced of, because you know those from whom you learned it, and how from infancy you have known the Holy Scriptures, which are able to make you wise for salvation through faith in Christ Jesus. (vv. 14–15)

I saw in myself a contrast between the "impostor" I had created and the person I truly was. The moment of my daughter's birth flashed through my mind, and the promise I had made to give her the father I never had.

I turned on the shower, turned out the lights, and I got down on my hands and knees and prayed, "God, I don't want to be like this anymore, but I don't know any other way. If you are real, please show yourself to me. Please, help me." I pleaded.

What happened next was a kind of visionary trance. I was caught somewhere between a dream and reality. I could see myself as a newborn, abandoned, never held, the little boy watching his mother walk away. Then I watched myself commit every sin in my life, one by one. As I viewed each sin, I repented and wept.

As my soul seemed to be vomiting out evil, I suddenly experienced a terrifying presence. A being of tremendous power was in the shower with me. In the total darkness of the room, there was a glowing. The darkness became like the daylight. My first reaction was absolute panic and fear. My soul was saying, "Please don't hurt me." In response to the panic, this being hugged me. It's the only way I can describe it. And I was embraced by warmth and light.

It was Jesus, and he was saying, "I love you. I'm not here to hurt you." Not with an audible voice, but through wordless communication right into my soul. I collapsed in that embrace and wept.

Eventually, the warmth and the presence left, I came back to reality, and the shower water, which had gone cold long before, felt like snowflakes on my naked body. I turned off the water and just lay there in a fetal position, shivering and trying to process what had just happened.

Once I was able to get up, I dressed and went to my grandmother. There she was, in the old pink chair, from which she prayed for me daily, smoked cigarettes, and tried to win my customers to

Christ. I said, "Grandma, I just met Jesus." I laid my head in the lap of the only person who truly loved me and cried, trying to explain what had just happened. "I'm so sorry for all the ways I've hurt you," I said.

She was shaken. She cried with me and simply said, "Praise God."

I wish I could say that things got better from this moment, but they didn't.

6

SEEING THE FACE OF GOD

He is the image of the invisible God, the firstborn of all creation.
Colossians 1:15

"To love another person is to see the face of God." So sings the chorus in the epilogue scene of Victor Hugo's *Les Misérables*.

Sadly, by most accounts, Hugo didn't know this firsthand. The French poet, novelist, and dramatist of the Romantic movement enjoyed a literary career that spanned more than sixty years. Both a graphomaniac and an erotomaniac, Hugo engaged in sexual relationships outside his marriage with a wide variety of women of all ages throughout his life—courtesans, actresses, prostitutes, admirers, servants, and revolutionaries.[1]

For more than fifty years, one of these women, Juliette Drouet, devoted her life to Hugo and even followed him into exile. She wrote some twenty thousand letters in which she expressed her passion or vented her jealousy on her womanizing lover. Hugo left his children a note regarding Juliette that read, "J.D. She saved my life in December 1851. For me she underwent exile. Never has her soul forsaken mine. Let those who have loved me love her. Let those who have loved me respect her. She is my widow."[2] And yet, even after his wife's death, Hugo never married Juliette or even remained monogamous. He was loved, but did he ever learn to love another? Did Hugo ever "see the face of God," as he so eloquently expressed?

Being loved can change the trajectory of our lives.

We can only love because we were first loved by God. And it's only in learning to love others that we can truly thrive as human beings. Jesus instructs us to make one focus the burning passion of our lives: "You shall love the Lord your God with all your heart, and with all your soul, and with all your strength, and with all your mind; *and your neighbor as yourself*" (Luke 10:27 NRSV, emphasis added).

Loving our neighbor is not some add-on, but the B-side of the same record. The twofold challenge of loving God and loving people made in the image of God is the lifelong pursuit of Christians.

It may be obvious why someone like Charles Manson would go down a path that ultimately led to murder. But what about those who seem to have been adequately loved and cared for?

In the early 1990s, the world watched the ongoing trial of two brothers who brutally murdered their own parents. Their father was a wealthy entertainment executive. They lived in a Beverly Hills mansion formerly inhabited by famous musicians such as Elton John and Prince. The two brothers enjoyed a kind of jet-setting life of the superrich.

On the evening of August 20, 1989, Lyle Menendez and his brother, Erik, went into the den, where their parents were sitting on the couch, and shot them to death with a Mossberg 12-gauge shotgun. Their parents were left unrecognizable from the gunshot wounds. The brothers staged the scene to look like a home invasion connected to organized crime. Within six months of the murders, they had spent an estimated one million dollars of their inheritance. Growing suspicion around their activities led to their arrest.

Their defense attorney claimed that Erik and Lyle were sexually abused by their father, and when they had finally reached a breaking point, they responded by brutally murdering both parents. The defense strategy failed because of overwhelming evidence that the Menendez parents were by all accounts a loving couple who provided everything for their boys. The Menendez brothers are now serving life imprisonment with multiple failed attempts to challenge the sentence.

It is not within the parameters of this book to offer a discussion on the crime and trial of the Menendez brothers, mental illness, or the underlying forces that can drive someone to commit heinous crimes, even against their own loved ones. Yet it is a prevalent theme throughout our human story that people who are loved and cared for can be quite capable of harming others. (See: Cain, in Genesis 4.)

Fred Rogers observed, "There's the good guy and the bad guy in all of us."[3] Good people can do bad things. Or as Rev. Dr. Martin Luther King Jr. once said, "There is some good in the worst of us and some evil in the best of us. When we discover this, we are less prone to hate our enemies."[4]

People can be loved, nurtured, and provided all the resources for human thriving, and still cause harm. People can be loved and never learn to love others.

True healing can only be found in learning to love.

Before I encountered Jesus in the shower, I had seen the face of God in my grandmother. She loved me unconditionally, and as Jesus began to heal my wounded heart, I learned to love her back.

After raising my head out of her lap, weeping together the night of my awakening, I became committed to pursuing this new life in Christ. That Sunday I went to church for the first time in years. I stood up in front of the congregation during the joys and concerns time and tried to report what had happened to me. There were audible gasps of relief, amens, and then applause.

Pastor Dan, the fedora-wearing, Indiana Jones–esque pastor from the shoot-out, took me in his office. He said, "Michael, I'm glad that Jesus has saved your soul, but AA will save your ass. Can you meet me at the noon meeting tomorrow?"

I didn't even know what Alcoholics Anonymous was. But I certainly wasn't going to waste my time with it. I had another plan. I was going back to the streets, to my associates, friends, and even enemies, and I was going to tell them about Jesus. I would tell them what had happened to me and that they needed to come join me at church.

Inspired by the film *The Prince of Egypt*, I drove to Daytona Beach, my old favorite place of sin and debauchery. In the place where MTV held spring break celebrations, the place where I would wake up after days of blackout, in bed with strangers, I walked out into the ocean, and I threw my gold chains and teeth into the sea. It was symbolic for me. I was throwing off the impostor as Moses had thrown off the trappings of Egypt in the desert.

I came back to Ocala and hit the streets. I passed out tracts and led new converts through the "sinner's prayer." Pastor Dan made me the youth pastor. I started bussing in inner-city kids from the local projects. We went from no youth group to a multiethnic group of thirty to forty kids and youth, many experiencing poverty and from broken homes.

I enrolled in college and started taking courses. I went legit, turning my tree service, which had started as a cover-up, into a lucrative corporation. What started with a truck, chain saw, and handful of drug addicts became a fleet of dump trucks, grapple trucks, and thirteen employees, doing major land-clearing contracts for new housing developments.

My wife at that time was not really on board with this newfound life. We had met when I was a drug dealer, which had been my most endearing quality to her. Nevertheless, I pushed forward, started preaching my first sermons, and realized I was called to ministry. My relationship with Gram became stronger than ever. She essentially raised my two daughters, and I would come home excited to share with her all that I was learning in school, as well as ministry and business updates.

One evening, just before I was preparing to graduate with an associate degree in psychology, I came home to find my grandmother slumped over in a chair. She had lost all bodily control and was unresponsive. I scooped her up in my arms and hauled it to the hospital. She had had an aneurism. For four months, she remained unresponsive. The doctors tried last-ditch surgeries, like the ventriculostomy, drilling a hole in her skull to let the fluids drain off her brain. They told me she wouldn't make it, but somehow, she did.

I had never prayed harder in my life. I believed that God would heal her. I moved into her hospital room. I stayed by her side night and day. I left for school and work but came right back. When I left, I would put headphones on her and play Andrew Scourby reading the King James Version of the Bible, her favorite. I studied by her side, ate hospital food, helped the nurses care for her, and begged God for a miracle.

The miracle did come, but not in the way I expected it. The doctors and nurses told me that she would never wake up and that I needed to prepare for her death. One night, as I was caressing her hand and face, I saw a vision. She was walking up over a hill, and on the other side was a multitude of people who had come out of a garden city of light to greet her. I said, "Momma, I love you, I know you are fighting for me. I'm going to be okay. You can let go."

Within an hour of my speaking those words, her body began to convulse. I held her in my arms as she died. It was just she and me together. After she had flatlined for some time, the nurses came in to console me. I couldn't let go of her body. She was growing cold and stiff, and I was still clinging to her. The nurses were trying gently to remove me, but I was frozen in fear, panic, and pain. The fear I had carried as a ten-year-old boy, burying my grandpa/father, was now fully realized.

Something died inside me there beside that hospital bed. I've never been the same to this day. I was angry at God, and my fundamentalist views only made it worse: "Come on, God. I turned my life around. I've done what you asked. I prayed and had faith like the Bible says. Why didn't you heal her, God?"

Soon my anger turned into rebellion: "You know what, God? If this is how you show your love, I'm done with you."

I envisioned Jesus on the cross, hanging there dead. I said, "Hey motherfucker, if you're real, you better come down off that cross and stop me, because I'm about to raise hell."

He didn't come off the cross. And I did raise hell.

My old friends were waiting for me. They had loved my grandma and had called her "Grams," their spiritual matriarch. One of my buddies slipped me an OxyContin. In my four-year run of recovery with the "Jesus cure," the drug landscape had changed. Cocaine was dead. In the 2000s, prescription pain medication was the new epidemic. That little pill, a "painkiller," was perfect for me. It "killed" emotional and physical pain, but it also killed me. When you use a large enough dose of opioid narcotics, you go into a blackout. It's called "nodding out." It's the closest you can get to death without dying. It takes you to a state of un-life. The lights are on, but no one is home. The pulse if there, but the person is gone. This is suicide as a process, rather than as a single act.

This started a four-year reign of terror. I was worse than ever before, going to depths of depravity I could have never imagined.

Director Alex Gibney's four-hour documentary "The Crime of the Century" (2020) exposes the magnitude of the opioid crisis. It pulls back the curtain on the underworld of Big Pharma, corrupt politicians, and government regulations that enabled the overproduction, reckless distribution, and abuse of synthetic opiates. Some called OxyContin "hillbilly heroin," and Florida was the epicenter of the crisis. Pill mills sprang up by the hundreds all over the state. Interstate 75, which runs from south Florida to the northeastern point of the Upper Peninsula of Michigan, became known as the "Oxy Highway." People came from all over the country to take advantage of largely unregulated pharmacies and dirty doctors. I was mixed up in the middle of it all.

I descended into this wonderful world of "doctor shopping" and jumped in with both feet. My friends and I took people into the known doctors with fake and altered MRIs and coached them on what to say. We could get thousands of pills, semi-illegally, at a time. The greatest "dope boys" of this era were legitimate doctors with medical degrees. And the pharmaceutical companies were the real "kingpins."

I became addicted to opiates to the point that I woke up dope sick and had to use just to get out of bed. I could function as the CEO of my company as long as I had dope, but when I ran out, I was deathly sick. I called this being a "functional drug addict." I could function just fine . . . as long as I had an opiate.

During this time, I had two sons, Michael and Alexander, with my ex-wife. The opiates refueled my old and primary addiction to sex. In the mornings I would set up my tree crews. The land-clearing contracts for major housing developments required us to come in and clear the pad for homes to be built. During the day, I would rent hotel rooms. While my wife was at home with the kids, I would gather with girlfriends and get high and have sex all day. When my wife and I finally split up, I went all in with this activity and didn't need to conceal it anymore. I bought a home that typically had three to five women living in it at all times, each of whom I was having sexual relationships with.

My four children from my first marriage grew up in this home and called many different women "Mom." Customers came night and day to buy pain pills from me. If the women were dope sick and didn't have money, I would have sex with them for a fix. My sex addiction progressed to multiple partners a day, wherever we could meet up, while my crews were working jobsites. At night, I would have sex while watching pornography, and then finish with mastur-bation. Opiates also inhibit the ability to climax during sex, so it's like a sex drug on steroids. Sometimes I went days without sleep.

I would go weeks at a time like this, not sleeping, snorting thou-sands of milligrams of OxyContin every day. Sometimes I would wake up in a blackout on the side of the road with my kids screaming in the background. Other times I woke up from a blackout in bed with women I didn't know. There were also many occasions when I woke up in a place with strangers who were plotting to rob me, or in a neighborhood where I would have to ask strangers what city I was in and what day it was.

The woman who had taught me to love had died. I used this as an excuse to dive into a downward spiral of addiction and suicide on the installment plan. In his book *Let Your Life Speak*, author and educator Parker Palmer shares that his "true self" emerged when he had finished wrestling with his "shadow-self," that deep depression that pushed him to the ground. He says, "I now know myself to be a person of weakness and strength, liability and giftedness, darkness and light. I now know that to be whole means to reject none of it but to embrace all of it." Palmer's insight that the "way to God is down" has certainly been true for me.[5]

It wasn't until I went fully down that I found God's infilling presence. I learned the hard way that sometimes when the world breaks our hearts open, God uses the cracks to gain entry inside. God now uses the struggles of my past to speak intimately to the abandonment, brokenness, and struggles in the lives of the people I serve.[6] Or as Nadia Bolz-Weber so eloquently says, "God makes beautiful things out of even my own shit."[7] It was only when I was finally whipped, rendered powerless, and left as a shattered shell of a human being that I finally saw "the face of God."

Ultimately, it was the love of another person that would awaken me from that living hell. A "broken hallelujah" kind of love.

7

A BROKEN HALLELUJAH

The sacrifice acceptable to God is a broken spirit; a broken and contrite heart, O God, you will not despise.
Psalm 51:17 NRSV

If there was ever a man who had it all, it was the biblical David. Not only did he have charisma, looks, intelligence, and ability, but he used those gifts for the betterment of his people. He was legendary as a lover and a fighter, a poet, a scholar, a warrior, and a brilliant military strategist. He was handpicked by God as an obscure shepherd boy in a family with seven older brothers to become the king of his people. And he ruled with integrity, wisdom, and humility. He was a devoted seeker and follower of God, which made him a leader of multitudes.

Now, as the king, David enjoyed unparalleled wealth. He unified the tribes, consolidated power, and ruled his people justly. His military, battle-hardened from decades of victories, were loyal to him alone. His people, once considered an unorganized group of escaped slaves, known for internal squabbles and divisions, had become a real kingdom. The obscure God they worshiped, YHWH, was now recognized as a legitimate divine being. The religious system was strengthened by his leadership.

David deeply loved his family, treating them with dignity and respect. His vision for the kingdom was one of justice for the lowly and oppressed and peace between all the peoples of the earth.

His building projects were massive. He left the city of Hebron to build a settlement on a hilltop, vacated ruins left by his enemy.

The city of Jerusalem was expanding more and more every day. The establishment of this new capital was one way he could unify the tribes of Israel. He dreamed of building a temple on top of Mount Moriah, the site where his ancestor Abraham had bound his beloved son Isaac, willing to sacrifice him there. This city on the mountainside would later become associated with his own name: the City of David. It became one of the most historically significant cities in the world.

But in 2 Samuel 11–12, we read a fateful tale . . .

Winter had passed, and with the spring came war. It was customary that the king would join the ranks on the battlefield. On this particular evening he decided to stay back. He had been fighting one war after another since he became the boy who stepped forth to slay the giant Goliath. Perhaps he was feeling a bit of entitlement. After all, he was the king now. Hadn't he spent enough time sweating and bleeding on the front lines?

He stood on his roof in the moonlight, peering over the incredible architectural feat that was Jerusalem. As he marveled at the wonders of the night life, the smells of dinner, and the chatter in the streets, something—someone—caught his eye.

She was bathing on a rooftop. Even from a distance, he could see her beauty, long flowing hair cascading down her voluptuous figure. He was smitten. He knew it was wrong to keep watching, but he couldn't take his eyes off of her. She was perhaps the most beautiful woman he had ever seen. He had to know who she was, so he sent his servants to summon her.

When she arrived, her beauty was even more stunning up close and personal. Her name was Bathsheba, and she was the wife of Uriah the Hittite, one of David's most faithful soldiers. His conscience fought against him. To commit adultery was a great sin in the eyes of God, and as the king, he would essentially be committing an act of power rape. Further, to sleep with the wife of one of his most faithful warriors would be nothing short of diabolical.

The spirit was strong, but the flesh was weak. Even as these thoughts were playing through his mind, he was seducing, wooing, and before long, having intercourse with Bathsheba. As soon as the deed was done, the shame and guilt came like an avalanche over David's soul. He sent her home.

As the days passed, he tried to forget about the encounter. He swept it under the rug of his soul. But weeks later, Bathsheba sent word that she was pregnant, with a message like the shrill voice of a daytime talk show host: "*You* are the father." David's guilt and shame came rushing back. What if people found out that he had committed adultery? It was a capital offense, punishable by execution. He had sat as judge of others for adultery and followed the letter of the law. Now would he himself be judged accordingly for the same sin? Even if he was somehow given mercy, he would lose his reputation and his crown.

He had to cover up his misdeeds at all costs. So, he hatched a truly clandestine plan. He would bring Uriah back from the front lines of the battlefield and send him home to sleep with Bathsheba. Then her pregnancy could be attributed to her husband.

He had Uriah brought to the palace.

"Uriah, my faithful warrior, how is General Joab, and how are the soldiers doing in the midst of the war?" David asked.

"They are well, my king. We destroyed the Ammonites and besieged Rabbah. All whom we encounter bow before your might, or we destroy them."

"Very well, my faithful warrior. Go down to your house and wash your feet." David was really encouraging Uriah to go home and enjoy the pleasures of his wife. He even sent a gift to Uriah's home to encourage the celebration of their union. But Uriah, faithful soldier of the king, was at war. He slept at the entrance to the palace among David's servants and did not go home at all.

The next morning a servant brought David a message: Uriah had not gone home to his wife. David brought Uriah in and asked him, "Haven't you just come from a military campaign? Why didn't you go home?"

"The ark and Israel and Judah are staying in tents, and my commander, Joab, and my lord's men are camped in the open country. How could I go to my house to eat and drink and make love to my wife? As surely as you live, I will not do such a thing!" Uriah protested.

David tried not to show the desperation that was bubbling up inside him. This faithful warrior, following the example of David's own integrity, would not break his vow to the king's service in the middle of a war.

In utter frustration, David said, "Stay here one more day, and tomorrow I will send you back." That night David invited Uriah to a feast. He served him the choicest of wines until Uriah became intoxicated. In their drunken revelry, David placed his hand on Uriah's shoulder, "Uriah, you have served me well. Now go home and enjoy the company of your wife. You can go back to the battlefield tomorrow. I'm your king, and this is my will for you." But again, Uriah did not go home. He went out to sleep on his mat among David's servants.

David, his back against the wall, called in his servant the next morning. The king wrote a letter to Joab and sent it with Uriah. It read, "Put Uriah out in front, where the fighting is fiercest. Then withdraw from him so he will be struck down and die." As soon as the faithful soldier departed his company, David withdrew to his chamber to weep.

Back on the battlefield, Joab was pressing the attack and had the city under siege. As instructed, he put Uriah at a place in the battle where he knew the strongest defenders were. When the opposing forces came out to defend the wall, Joab pulled back. Uriah the Hittite was killed.

A messenger was sent to deliver the news to Bathsheba of her husband's death. She went through the customary period of mourning for him. As soon as the grieving period was over, a servant of David knocked on her door. "The king summons you. He desires to make you his wife." Bathsheba accepted the invitation. She and David were married, and the child of their adulterous affair was born.

David, the shepherd boy, handpicked by God to be king of Israel.

David, slayer of giants.

David, a "man after God's own heart" (see Acts 13:22), had become an adulterer, power rapist, murderer, and a mafia-like boss, ordering a hit on his faithful commander. Oh, how the mighty had fallen. The king sought to conceal the whole matter, and for a time, no one knew of the entire affair.

No one but God.

God sent his prophet Nathan to David, and Nathan told David a little story: There were two men in a town. One had everything and the other had nothing. The wealthy man, with his many sheep and cattle, decided to take the poor man's only little ewe lamb, which was like a daughter to him. The rich man, rather than drawing from his abundance, took the one little lamb the poor man had to feed a visitor. Nathan let the story hang for a while.

David was infuriated. "As surely as the Lord lives, the man who did this must die! He must pay for that lamb four times over, because he did such a thing and had no pity," he growled.

Nathan paused, looked deep into the eyes of the king, and said, "*You* are the man!"

David immediately fell to his knees, the weight of his sin pressing down.

The Lord, speaking through the prophet Nathan, let David know that because of his sin, there would be hell to pay in his own home, and worse, that his newborn son would die.

David repented and pleaded for mercy. His confession is recorded in Psalm 51, in which David begs, "Create in me a clean heart, O God, and put a new and right spirit within me. . . . The sacrifice acceptable to God is a broken spirit; a broken and contrite heart, O God, you will not despise" (vv. 10, 17).

This poem of repentance has become the heart cry of every desperate sinner who recognizes the weight of his or her sin and the inability to make recompense for that evil. It is one of the most hopeful passages in the entire Bible.

Nathan let David know that he would not receive what the law required, which was death. He would receive mercy. There would be grace, but the consequences of his sin were inescapable. God's forgiveness does not mean the consequences of sin magically disappear.

Hell was unleashed, indeed. Not only did David lose his son, but children in his own house revolted against him. While he was never removed from leadership, his life from that point forward was a constant struggle of deceptive plots and family dysfunction. The life he had known was burned to the ground.

But there was hope in the ashes.

There was a hallelujah, but it was a cold and broken hallelujah.

David and Bathsheba seemed to fall deeply in love. From the atrocity of David's sin, something good emerged. Together they had another child, Solomon. It was Solomon who became the next king of Israel, and it was Solomon, not David, who would build the Lord's house on that mountain overlooking Jerusalem. He became known as the wisest king ever to rule. He took a destabilized nation, coming apart under his father's care, and brought it back to health and stability again.

Yet, Solomon too, had his own dark side, his own ashes.

That the child of David and Bathsheba, a marriage that had started with murder, espionage, and adultery, became the next king is significant. But it doesn't stop there. There would be another great king who would come from that adulterous union. The greatest king who ever was, the One before whom every nation would bow, the one called "King of kings."

Fast-forward to a single obscure reference in Matthew's genealogy of Jesus, which reads, ". . . Jesse the father of King David. David was the father of Solomon, whose mother had been Uriah's wife" (Matt 1:6). It's as if Matthew can't even say her name, hundreds of years later. She is just known as "Uriah's wife."

But her name was Bathsheba. And the Old Testament insisted that the prophesied Messiah would come through the lineage of David. The way that happened was through the womb of Bathsheba, then Solomon, the love child of a king's adulterous affair.

We say "hallelujah" to this Messiah, this King of kings, but it is always a broken hallelujah.

I've spent a great deal of time wondering about this. Why did God choose this route, to become incarnate through this particular lineage? The only conclusion I can reach is that God likes to paint with ashes. God doesn't waste anything. God can use even our moments of epic failure in redemptive ways for others.

We can look at David and say, "What in the world was wrong with this guy? He had it all, and he threw it away for a one-night stand?" Yet perhaps we should not be so quick to judge. David and Bathsheba's story is *our* story. We too have been given the treasures of heaven, and we too have had our moments of failure, concealment, and ultimate desperation. Or in the words of C. S. Lewis, "It would seem that Our Lord finds our desires not too strong, but too weak. We are half-hearted creatures, fooling about with drink and sex and ambition when infinite joy is offered us, like an ignorant child who wants to go on making mud pies in a slum because he cannot imagine what is meant by the offer of a holiday at the sea. We are far too easily pleased."[1]

Somehow, in the ashes of it all, God brought forth the Savior of the world, a Savior whose genealogy traces back to an adulterous affair with "Uriah's wife."

A Savior conceived out of wedlock in the womb of a virgin named Mary. A highly suspect story indeed for the local townsfolk.

A Savior who ate with "tax collectors and sinners" (Matt 9:10–11).

A Savior who rode into the poor side of town, among the marginalized and oppressed, on a donkey.

A Savior in whom we see the face of God emerging from a genealogical mess.

A Savior who died on a cross to take away the sins of the world. In Jesus, the cross, the greatest symbol of suffering and shame, becomes a symbol of hope and glory. The ultimate moment of weakness and vulnerability reveals the cruciform shape of God's omnipotent power. Nowhere is it more apparent than at the cross . . . *that God paints with ashes.*

The cross is a hallelujah moment indeed, but it is a broken hallelujah.

The phrase "broken hallelujah" comes from Canadian singer-songwriter, poet, and novelist Leonard Cohen's most famous song,

"Hallelujah." The song has been expressed in many other arrangements by multiple artists, with more than three hundred versions performed on recordings and in concerts, films, and television soundtracks. It resurged in popularity among emerging generations after being featured in the 2001 film *Shrek*. Sadly, in a post-Christian world, many are unaware of the biblical references to David and Bathsheba, as well as Samson, or the reality that hallelujahs come in many forms.

Cohen, a Sabbath-observing Jew, reportedly wrote eighty draft verses for the song, including one writing session at the Royalton Hotel in New York, where he was reduced to sitting on the floor in his underwear, banging his head on the floor. Painting with ashes indeed. Cohen said of Jesus:

> I'm very fond of Jesus Christ. He may be the most beautiful guy who walked the face of this earth. Any guy who says "Blessed are the poor. Blessed are the meek" has got to be a figure of unparalleled generosity and insight and madness . . . A man who declared himself to stand among the thieves, the prostitutes, and the homeless. His position cannot be comprehended. It is an inhuman generosity. A generosity that would overthrow the world if it was embraced because nothing would weather that compassion. I'm not trying to alter the Jewish view of Jesus Christ. But to me, in spite of what I know about the history of legal Christianity, the figure of the man has touched me.[2]

Cohen expresses the sentiments of many "spiritual but not religious" people today—utterly captivated by Jesus yet utterly opposed to the organized religion that bears his name. In some way, we can all find ourselves in times of broken hallelujahs.

Ubuntu. We are interconnected with this story; it flows through our veins. I for one am grateful. This story gives me great hope as a sinner of King David proportions. Will God bring great healing to generations to come through my greatest failures? Will God take our ashes and bring forth wounded healers? Can God bring forth redemption from love born of an adulterous affair?

I was sitting at the Circle K gas station on Southwest 200 in Ocala, Florida, just past noon. Then I saw her.

My crew foreman had sent me to bring his paycheck to his wife. She needed to pay a bill. He needed to press the men toward finishing a big job. I agreed to handle the errand. She jumped out of a green minivan. She was wearing a pink top and jeans. She had long, curly blonde hair and bright green eyes. I leaned up against my car in my usual white tee, sagging jeans, with J's on my feet (aka Nike Air Jordans).

As she approached the car, I was struck. She was so beautiful that I was taken aback and speechless. I could only muster one word: "Damn!" Her jaw dropped for a moment in shock and disbelief.

"Are you his boss?" she asked.

"Yep." I was looking her up and down in a completely inappropriate way.

"You got his check?" she interrogated.

"Yep." I handed it over to her.

"Thank you." She turned and started walking back to the minivan, but not before turning back to flash a mischievous little smile.

"Your name is Jill?" I asked as she jumped into the driver's seat. Her girlfriends were giggling in the car.

"That's right." She smiled as she put the car in reverse and proceeded to back out.

That's how I met my Bathsheba. I was completely sprung. Already in my mind, I was plotting how I could find a way to meet up with her again. It wasn't just her beauty, but how she interacted, how she smiled, how she could turn and walk away. There was an odd and immediate soul connection.

To paraphrase Marius in *Les Misérables*, I was singing:

> Had you seen her today,
> You might know how it feels
> When what was right seems wrong,
> and what was wrong seems right!"[3]

Sadly, I was a kind of professional mate-poacher at the time. I had a whole harem of women living in my house, some of whom were married to other people. I had no moral compass.

My foreman, Jill's husband, was a big dude. His street name was "6'9." He used to break people's kneecaps for one of the local drug kingpins. So, I was a bit worried that she would tell him about our interaction.

She didn't. Over the next several weeks, we had several more "chance encounters." Chance as in manufactured by me, when I knew that she would be on a jobsite to pick him up or drop him off for work. A few days later she was on-site, waiting for us to finish a job, so I took my shirt off, grabbed a chain saw, and starting working circles around my crew. It was all a show for her.

Next time she needed his paycheck, she called my cell phone. Boom! The world had just changed!

Jill and I started to have an affair.

Her husband struggled with a serious crack addiction. He was also abusive toward and had several affairs of his own going on. I frequently took him out to the club and set him up with girls I knew. He and I were in the throes of addiction. We were brothers in bondage to a shared master. He was a friend, and I let him move into my house for a while. But that didn't stop me from going after Jill. Ultimately, he found out. Our relationship fragmented, and he quit working for me. Jill stayed.

Jill wasn't impressed with the four women living in my home, or the others who stayed over certain nights during the week. She started running these girls off one by one, strategically cleaning house. Jill started off as my "nanny." She took care of the kids, made dinner, and brought me coffee in the mornings. Meanwhile, the last of my live-in girlfriends, who also worked at the day care where I took my sons, was dragging me to church each week. She was Dominican, and the church she took me to was conducted in Spanish. I had no idea what they were saying, but I know they prayed over me a lot.

At the time, I was actually considering trying to get clean. My addiction had gotten to the place where I didn't even get high anymore. I had to take more than a thousand milligrams of OxyContin every day just to function. But there was no actual effect anymore. This is the insanity of addiction. You chase a high you can no longer achieve, but because of the phenomenon of dependency and tolerance, you end up simply using to avoid getting sick.

Jill decided to take the clothes of the last woman standing out of my closet and throw them outside into the woods. After a heated verbal altercation, it was only Jill who was left. She moved in and has never moved out since. She has three children from her previous marriage, and I have four (there was another one out there I didn't know about at the time, but that's for later). I had custody of my four, and she had custody of her three. Together we blended a family of seven kids.

Jill was a "party girl" but didn't do drugs. We would go to the club several times a week. I would purchase the VIP room and bottle service. She could throw down drink for drink with me, and we would dance, have fun, and party until I would go into blackout mode.

Very early in our relationship, I started to fall in love with Jill. We started with "lust at first sight," but that had evolved into love. She was a good mother. She wasn't a drug addict, like every other woman I knew. And I could feel that she loved me. She looked at the college diploma on my wall and the memorabilia from my youth pastor days, and she kept asking me how I had gone from that to who I was.

I was falling more and more in love with Jill. At some point, I decided that it was time to get clean. On several occasions, Jill locked me away at home so I could go through withdrawals. A couple of times I made it a day or two, but the symptoms got so bad that I caved. Next, we tried to see a doctor who would "cure" me, which also failed.

On some of those occasions, Jill held me in her arms, caressing me and rocking me, as I puked out poison and went through hallucinogenic states. Often during those times, I saw Jill as my grandmother, back from the dead, and we had conversations.

After all of that failed, I did the thing no junkie ever wants to do. I went to the methadone clinic. They tried a new "miracle drug" on me that had just came out, called Suboxone, but it only works if you stop getting high, something I couldn't do. They switched me to methadone. Every morning Jill drove to the clinic so I could wait at the window for my government-distributed dope. The methadone was so good I decided it was even better if I added hundreds of milligrams of OxyContin and Xanax on top of it. It turns out the thing that was supposed to help me get clean helped me achieve a high again. None of this is a good idea, you know, in view of potential death.

The thing about so-called replacement therapy is that it doesn't work. It is only a "replacement" for actual recovery. It basically produces state-raised drug addicts, for whom the clinic or "treatment center" becomes the new dope man. Methadone, a synthetic opioid agonist, was developed by German scientists in 1937. It was brought to market in 1943 and widely used by the Nazi army during World War II. Its use was discontinued after the discovery of severe side effects, some of which included dependency, tolerance, and withdrawal.

Ironically, there is no known worse opiate withdrawal than from methadone. Additionally, after extended use, it creates a dependency that other opiates can no longer effect. After a while, trying to get off of it is worse than trying to kick heroin or OxyContin.

Jill watched me try and fail to get clean over and over again, only to become a worse addict than ever before. As a "functional addict," someone who depended on a substance to not become sick, I was still running a company that generated good profits. My drug-dealing activities had basically just become a way to subsidize my own use. Despite these failures, Jill and I continued to work and raise our family.

For fun, we took our kids on weekend trips across Florida to the beach and amusement parks. On one of these trips, May 3, 2008, I prayed a dangerous prayer. That morning, I left Jill and the kids to go down to the Tampa methadone clinic to get my daily dose. I thought to myself how particularly screwed up it was that my family had to wait in a hotel room for Dad to go get his state-sponsored dope so they could enjoy a day in the amusement park.

That night I wrote a one-line entry in my journal: "God, whatever you need to do to stop me, please do it." Jill and I got down on our knees in front of the bed in that hotel room, and we prayed together for the first time. I spoke out the line from my journal, concluding with "Please stop me." The words resonated into eternity and landed on the throne of God.

That was a dangerous prayer. Be careful what you pray for, as they say.

The next day, God sent angels in green suits with handcuffs to answer my prayer.

8

ANGELS IN GREEN SUITS
WITH HANDCUFFS

Even though you intended to do harm to me,
God intended it for good, in order to preserve a numerous
people, as he is doing today.
Genesis 50:20

Martin Luther King Jr. was a black child growing up in the south of a segregated United States. One year in junior high, he participated in a public speaking contest and won the prize. As he rode home on the bus, the bus driver forced him and his black teacher to give up their seats to accommodate the white folks getting on. At first he resisted, but finally, his teacher convinced him to give up his seat. This situation frustrated the young King to no end, and he described it as "the angriest I had ever been in my life." Why was he considered less of a person simply due to the color of his skin? That childhood experience, which wounded him deeply, also helped shape his passion in later life.

As he grew up, he pursued and achieved the highest level of education possible. Because he excelled as a student, he skipped several grades and graduated early. He started at Morehouse College at just fifteen years old, where he earned a bachelor of arts. He earned a master of divinity from Crozer Theological Seminary, then finally a doctorate in systematic theology from Boston University in 1955, at the age of just twenty-six.

It seemed King was chosen for a special vocation with implications beyond the local congregation. On December 1, 1955, Rosa Parks, another African American, was arrested for violating segregation laws when she rejected a bus driver's order to vacate her seat for a white passenger in Montgomery, Alabama. In the wake of this event, King was asked to provide leadership and thus arose "the Moral Leader" of the nation.[1]

As the newly elected leader of the Montgomery Improvement Association (MIA), Martin Luther King Jr. coordinated the Montgomery bus boycott, a thirteen-month mass protest. In the struggle for civil rights, King was arrested numerous times. On February 21, 1956, a Montgomery grand jury indicted King and other MIA leaders for violating the anti-boycott law. King was found guilty and sentenced to a $500 fine or 386 days in jail. The case was appealed and ultimately led to the U.S. Supreme Court ruling that segregation on public buses was unconstitutional. He became a prominent civil rights leader and harnessed the power of nonviolent mass protest to successfully challenge racial segregation.

On April 16, 1963, during one of his incarcerations, King wrote an open letter titled "Letter from Birmingham Jail," one of the most inspired and powerful pieces of literature ever produced. In it he articulated that citizens have a moral responsibility to break unjust laws when they are oppressive to some groups of people, calling on them to take direct action rather than wait for a justice that may never materialize. He called out his fellow clergyman for not bringing their bodies and voices to the struggle. "Injustice anywhere" he wrote, "is a threat to justice everywhere."[2] The letter is read and studied each year by millions of people. It is a foundational document for those engaged in the work of antiracism and social justice.

Each of King's arrests and imprisonments only further catalyzed and propelled the movement for racial equality.

In the famous speech we now call "I Have a Dream," King celebrated the glory of America's constitutional democracy, but (re) signed it in a way that forced his audience to rethink America's commitment to its own ideals. King was able to navigate honoring the legitimating narrative of the past, while exposing its inconsistencies.

He gave voice to the struggles of an oppressed people, yet in a way that the oppressor could hear in a non-retaliatory manner.[3]

Was King carrying a dream in his soul since the moment he was forced out of his seat on that bus? Is it possible he was using the pain he had carried all his life now to bring freedom, equality, and healing to others?

Martin Luther King Jr. painted with ashes, and the world has been forever changed.

Throughout history, and particularly in the life of King, we can see how randomness, disorder, and the chaos of a moment can lead to large-scale healing and renewal. I have been a student of Dr. King in my own preaching and leadership for years. I believe that King is an embodied witness of the kind of leadership the church needs today. He successfully navigated a time of seismic shifts. While he aptly voiced his frustration with fellow clergy in his "Letter from Birmingham Jail," he never devolved into name-calling and attacks. King was able to see the structures of our faith that needed deconstruction without destroying the whole house.

If anyone would have been vindicated for resorting to attacking the systems of his day, it was King. However, he capably named the injustices faced by African American people, noting the church's complicity in those practices, while simultaneously lifting up a vision of hope for what could be. He exemplifies the kind of wounded healer it takes to lead a wounded nation on a journey toward healing.

In Genesis 50:20, the biblical Joseph says to his brothers, "Even though you intended to do harm to me, God intended it for good, in order to preserve a numerous people, as he is doing today" (NRSV). If anyone's life in modern times reflected that statement, it was Martin Luther King Jr.

In the story of Joseph, the boy's jealous brothers throw him into a pit and ultimately sell him into slavery to Egypt. Like King, Joseph was a dreamer. As the favored child of his father, born in a blended family to his father's favorite wife, Joseph was resented by his brothers. Later, in Egypt, he was falsely accused of attempted rape by his master's wife and ended up in prison, rotting away in a dungeon.

But even in that place of darkness, Joseph the dreamer used his gift of interpreting dreams among his fellow prisoners.

In time, Joseph was called upon to interpret the dreams of the pharaoh himself. After Pharaoh had a series of troubling dreams, one of Joseph's fellow former inmates, who had been restored to Pharaoh's court, informed the pharaoh of a prisoner who could interpret dreams. Though all of Pharaoh's court had failed to interpret the dreams, Joseph was able, and he went from prisoner to vice president of the most powerful nation in the ancient world in what seemed like a day. Pharaoh placed Joseph in a position of managing the affairs of the entire nation in the face of a coming famine. When Joseph's brothers, the ones who had harmed him, came before him begging for grain, he gave them mercy and forgiveness, rather than punishment (Genesis 50).

He gave them love in exchange for their hate.

Joseph's story demonstrates how God can bring great good even out of malicious intent and evil systems. God can work from within chaos and randomness. Somehow God is "with us" in the midst of it all. Most important, in the words of King, it teaches us that "darkness cannot drive out darkness; only light can do that. Hate cannot drive out hate; only love can do that."[4]

<hr />

I believe that somehow, God was at work in my circumstances as a desperate drug addict, discarded by my biological parents and orphaned by my grandparents' deaths.

God heard the prayer of desperation Jill and I prayed together in that hotel room in Tampa, Florida, "God, whatever you have to do to stop me, please do it." The next day I decided that I would not go to the methadone clinic that morning. I would start the first day of my new life. My bright idea was to just drink myself through the onset of withdrawals, then get back home for the night to cave out for a couple of days of detox.

At Busch Gardens, they had a "Hospitality House" where guests could go to get free beers throughout the day. I thought it was such a hospitable thing for them to do. I wanted to be a good guest, so I took them up on their hospitality. Jill and my children ended up without me most of the day, as I drank myself into a good buzz. After getting into it with one of the Hospitality House employees who thought I was taking advantage of their hospitality, I started stumbling around with the kids. Jill's feet were hurting, and her sandals were coming apart. I walked into a souvenir shop and picked out a perfect pair of new flip-flops, along with some candy and a bottle of Mountain Dew.

I brought Jill the new pair of sandals and tossed the kids the snacks. Then some nice gentleman grabbed me from behind and started placing my hands behind my back, letting me know that I was under arrest. First, I had apparently forgotten to pay for those sandals and items from the souvenir shop. Second, I was on felony house arrest out of Marion County, Florida, for pending cases related to my string of drug dealings and thefts. Being that I was in Hillsborough County with no formal permission, I was technically an illegal alien and an unwanted guest.

I watched my children's faces melt in horror as once again they watched their father being arrested. They screamed and wept and made a terrible scene. It seemed as if the whole park had stopped to watch the show. It was one of the most embarrassing and shameful moments of my life.

As the deputies were hauling my drunken self in, I said, "Come on, man. You're going to arrest me in front of my kids?" One of the deputies detaining me said, "Your kids are better off without you, you piece of shit."

I responded with a healthy "Fuck you," though I also thought that what he'd said was true.

I was booked and detained for felony extradition back to Marion County. I woke up in the Hillsborough County Jail, the luxurious Orient Road facility. It was May 5, Cinco de Mayo, and scores of Latino and Hispanic gang members were coming in to the jail. My withdrawals were starting to kick in. Fortunately, this particular jail gave inmates on methadone a step-down process. Marion County had four days to pick me up, or I had to be released. They showed up on the fourth day.

MCJ had a different philosophy. It prided itself on being a "no frills" jail.[5] That meant no commissary, no televisions, and no recreational activities. It sometimes meant no food, no mats, no pillow, no items of comfort. It also meant no help with your withdrawals. The MCJ policy is SAYL: Sorry About Your Luck.

During the intake I told the nurse I was taking hundreds of milligrams of methadone and OxyContin daily, as well as a little Xanax nightcap, but during the day. She gave me the SAYL classification and sent me to the general population. That's when I pulled my ace card. I pulled down my pants. Fortunately, the one thing I had going for me was a massive staph infection in my groin area. This bought me a ticket to a quarantined glass cell in the infirmary. If you're going to do cold turkey withdrawals from hundreds of milligrams of opioids, this was the place to do it.

A doctor came in to lance my infection in the most aggressive, don't-give-a-damn way and then began (occasionally) to monitor me. There, on the floor of the infirmary room, I spewed bile from every orifice. No meds. No real medical care. "No frills."

Thanks be to God it was just what I needed.

In the isolation of the quarantined cell, it was just me, demons, hallucinations, and of course . . . Jesus, the wounded Healer who sat with me in the silence. He held me and nurtured me back to health.

I ended up back in general population a week later, still going through massive withdrawals. I lay in my bunk for a month, getting up only to vomit or spew diarrhea. I couldn't eat. A couple of inmates brought me cups of water so I didn't die of dehydration. There is no withdrawal as terrible as methadone. I could feel it coming out of my bones for months.

At this stage in my criminal development, I had progressed to the point where I paid my lawyer in advance before I committed new crimes. He was able to convince the judge to give me a shot at work release, so I could support my family, run my business, and come stay in jail on the weekends. Because I was incarcerated so much, I had already built an elaborate system of smuggling in contraband, such as cigarettes and chewing tobacco. I also knew which guards were dirty and would work with me. I was placed out on the inmate work farm. One of the deputies took me in as his personal trustee. I got in his truck, and after we got down the road a ways, I could shed my stripes and break out my white tee, jeans, and cell phone. He kept these in his truck for me.

Our deal was that I got him anything he needed, and he provided my incarceration with a couple of "frills." I was able to run my business from jail, meet up with Jill to make exchanges, and be intimate. My nickname was "kingpin," because I supplied an entire section of the jail with tobacco products and lighters. Men piled trays of food in front of me morning, noon, and night. I had "mules" (prison slang for those who transport contraband into a facility), "suitcasing" (another prison term for carrying contraband packages in the rectum), and guards who let the system work. That was until a disgruntled fellow inmate snitched on me to the authorities. Just before I was about to be cleared for work release, a group of officers swarmed the truck I rode around in. They arrested me again for multiple counts of "introduction of contraband."

And there I went, back to Alpha pod, Charlie section. Hello, darkness, my old friend. Once again, I found myself in jail within jail: solitary confinement. The judge revoked my work release, Jill and the kids were crushed, but my lawyer got me a sweet one-year deal.

Finally, I had found my bottom.

I started to pray again, read the Bible, and go to recovery meetings in jail. Jill took care of our children that whole time. She never gave up on me, even when I managed to somehow screw up incarceration. She visited me. She wrote me. She was my companion in that cell. And when I finally walked out of that barbed-wire gate, she was waiting in the parking lot.

Sometimes God uses our worst mistakes to bring healing. God is not some micromanaging powermonger sitting on a cloud, doling out blessings and curses. But sometimes God sends angels in green suits with handcuffs as an answer to our prayers.

Incarceration breaks some people. Being placed in a cage like an animal can dehumanize us further, teaching us to hate. But others, like Dr. King and Joseph of Egypt, turned their cells into sanctuaries from which to interpret dreams and write sacred letters that transformed the world.

Sometimes a broken, racist system built on the backs of genocide and slavery turns in on itself. And God sends prophets to boldly proclaim subversive dreams of beauty in the ruin of ashes. One such a prophet stood in the smoldering ashes of his society and saw beauty. Amid the people of his tribe, ambling around in the dust of systemic racism, he heard a word from the Lord and proclaimed: "I have a dream that . . . with this faith we will be able to hew out of the mountain of despair a stone of hope."[6]

Martin Luther King Jr. exemplified the ability to "love your enemies." He once said, "Hate is too great a burden to bear. I have decided to love."[7] Love is a subversive counterforce to the narrative of control, exclusion, and domination. King tapped into people's pain of isolation and harnessed the nonviolent power of unconditional love. This created space for people who once stereotyped the *other* as a racial enemy to now enter the fullness of relationship as equals.

Joseph's loving forgiveness of his brothers brought healing and provision for his family. King possessed the inner resilience to continue to love in the face of hate. Both men changed the trajectory of nations. Both turned the death-dealing systems meant to harm them into bastions of healing. They used the pain of abandonment, minimization, and nullification to bring into reality new dreams of what could be. They transformed the trauma of their incarceration into beauty and hope for others.

The greatest wounded healers are those who know that what others meant for ill, God will use for good. They can pray, "Father, forgive them, for they do not know what they are doing."

Unconditional love is the power that transforms desperation into hope.

I saw the face of God for the first time in my wife, Jill Beck. She taught me how to give and receive love again. Our love was a broken hallelujah. But the Savior on a cross shined his face on us. That was fourteen years ago.

Learning to love Jill these past fourteen years has rescued me. We started ugly: blending a family of eight children, resurrecting a business, making amends, staying clean and sober. It has been a great challenge. But my wife, Jill Marie Beck, has loved me unconditionally. Her love saved me in more ways than one. It gave me a will to live again. Like David and Bathsheba's, our "lust at first sight" affair started in the ashes of our brokenness, and there was hell to pay. But God has been showing us how to paint with ashes ever since.

It was Jill's redeeming, sustaining, and unconditional love that brought me back from death. She gave me the courage to pray that dangerous prayer. In the safety of our relationship, I was free to receive and give love again. This flow of receiving and giving is the lifelong journey of becoming wounded healers.

I felt abandoned and betrayed, thrown into a pit by those who were supposed to love me. I was further warped by a system in which juvenile offenders were trained to be better criminals, dirty cops used my mother to set up drug dealers, and wealthy people with high-class attorneys could commit crimes and buy their way out of consequences. But God turned that very system in on itself to work out my redemption.

Sometimes God sends angels in green suits with handcuffs. It was while confined in a cell that I came to know freedom for the first time. The cell became a sanctuary where I first began to learn a new design for living.

PART THREE:
RESTORATION

9

DESIGN FOR LIVING

Therefore, in order to keep me from becoming conceited, I was given a thorn in my flesh, a messenger of Satan, to torment me. Three times I pleaded with the Lord to take it away from me. But he said to me, "My grace is sufficient for you, for my power is made perfect in weakness." Therefore, I will boast all the more gladly about my weaknesses, so that Christ's power may rest on me.

2 Corinthians 12:7–9

Saul of Tarsus had attained the highest education possible, apprenticing himself to the top scholar of his day. He was climbing the ranks of success in the world of religious leadership. He was on the way to a premier spot in the ruling religious body. His accolades, his prestige, and his obsessive perfectionism regarding the righteous upholding of Levitical law were impeccable (Phil 3:4–6).

Then he caught wind of an emerging heretical sect of Judaism, called the followers of "the Way." This group adhered to the laughable proposition that the Messiah of Israel had come and gone. The man of whom they spoke had been a rabble-rouser. He had defiled himself by associating with the unclean and had even made blasphemous claims about his own identity as the divine Son of God. Finally, he was crucified on a Roman cross, the lowest, most shameful form of execution, reserved for the basest of criminals, insurrectionists, and thieves. And *this* was the man this new sect called "Messiah."

Although it was his job, Saul also considered it his personal calling to stamp out this movement. In doing so he could both eliminate a dangerous heresy and improve his position climbing the ranks of religious power. He became a kind of "Dog the Bounty Hunter" of Christians, following leads, chasing them down, and hauling them in to be executed. That is, until Saul of Tarsus had a supernatural encounter with the very Jesus he was seeking to discredit.

On a road leading to Damascus, on his way to stamp out another group of heretical followers, Saul was thrown from his horse. Then, a bright light rendered him blind and helpless, and he was forced to fall into the care of the very Christians he sought to destroy. He came to know his gift of desperation in a profound way.

Under the care of a stranger named Ananias, a follower of the Way, his vision was restored, and a new name and vocation given. He became Paul, the apostle to the Gentiles. He traveled the known world, sharing the good news of this crucified and resurrected Jesus. The same instincts and character defects that had made him such a formidable foe of Christians throughout the Roman Empire turned him into the greatest proponent of the faith. Multiple incarcerations, stonings, shipwrecks, and near-death experiences couldn't stop him from painting with ashes. Ultimately, he was executed for his faith in the same way he had been involved with executing others.

Some hurt people who excel in hurting people have radical conversions to become healers. Saul of Tarsus was one such person. Perhaps what we can learn most from his life is what he did with his ashes. A careful reading of Paul's letters shows a man conflicted. Some of the most beautiful passages of the Bible come from his "outbox." However, we also may recognize some narcissism and a need to be recognized as a "real" apostle, like James, Mary, or Peter.

Even well into his journey as the "apostle to the Gentiles," we see an ongoing struggle in his soul. "I know the things I ought to do, but don't . . . Who will deliver me from this body of death?" (Rom 7:19, 25, paraphrased). Perhaps this premier Pharisaic scholar is using rhetorical devices to make his points more poignant. Yet, Paul describes an aspect of his ongoing struggle in his own words. Because of his superior intelligence, incredible giftings, and visions of the heavenly realm that many never saw, he was in the danger zone of becoming "conceited." So, in Paul's estimation, to keep himself in check, he was given a "thorn in [his] flesh," a messenger of Satan, to torment him.

When Paul pleads for the removal of this "thorn," Jesus responds with "My grace is sufficient for you, for my power is made perfect in weakness" (2 Cor 12:7–9).

Paul learned that his most exceptional qualities were paradoxically also his weaknesses, not his strengths. His journey of healing was not complete with his conversion experience. It was an ongoing journey. It was his woundedness that kept him leaning ever more fully into his dependence on Jesus. He was in a position of humble submission, completely reliant upon God's grace, a grace that was given one day at a time.

People who paint with ashes do so not because they are stronger than others, but because they are aware of their woundedness. Master ash-painting artists are those who know they are completely dependent upon the wounded healer: Jesus.

〰〰〰

The only thing you can cure is a ham.
—recovery cliché

Jesus once found a man lying among a community of blind, lame, and paralyzed people at the Pool of Bethesda by the Sheep Gate in Jerusalem, the great city of his ancestor David. This particular man had been ill for thirty-eight years. Jesus asked him, "Do you want to be made well?"

The man rattled off an excuse (real or perceived) about not being able to get down to the healing pool. Jesus told him to get up and walk, and immediately he did (John 5:1–9).

Jesus asks us all the same question, *"Do you want to be well?"*

We have to want healing. No one can give us the desire or do the work for us. Understanding our weaknesses as superpowers and our wounds as a source of healing is not about making excuses to stay sick in whatever form. To the contrary, it helps us understand that healing is a journey. Jesus doesn't typically "cure" us. Instead, he consistently heals us—one day at a time.

Every day we need a fresh encounter with Jesus. Every day we submit our weakness to him. As it did for the Israelites wandering in the wilderness, the "manna" of our healing comes one day at a time. As the Israelites learned in the wilderness, we can't store up for tomorrow. God gives us just enough for today because, as Jesus said, "each day has enough trouble of its own" (Matt 6:34). Every day we invite him to be the Lord of our lives. That means he's our Master, and our life is now under new management. Each day, we need to check in with the Boss. We yield our woundedness to him, and he in exchange gives us fresh grace. Each day, we turn to him, and he gives us the power to heal, a power made perfect in our weakness.

When I walked out of the MCJ after my prayer of desperation, something I had done many times before, I was committed to do two things. The first was go to St. Mark's Church and see Pastor Dan and the second was go to a meeting. Jill was there, waiting in the parking lot, when I was discharged. We ran and embraced, then left the jail and went straight to St. Mark's. I told Jill there was something I needed to do. Pastor Dan met me in the sanctuary and welcomed me with open arms. I said, "Hey Dan, remember when you told me that Jesus saved my soul, but AA could save my ass?"

"Yep." He grinned, beneath his fedora.

"I think you were right. Can I meet you at the nooner tomorrow?"

Our business was in shambles. A bunch of strung-out employees had robbed Jill blind. Days before my release, she was evicted. Her father and other family members had to help her just to provide food and shelter. We were homeless. I scraped enough money together to get a hotel room for us and our seven kids. The only vehicle we had broke down that day. We didn't let that stop us. A member of the fellowship came and picked me up and took me to a meeting. There, I stuck my hand in the air and said, "Hi, I'm Michael, and I'm an alcoholic/addict. I just got out of jail today. Again. I need help."

The room responded with, "Hi. Michael. Glad you're here. Keep coming back."

I did come back. Every day. And thirteen years later, I still keep coming back.

"Keep coming back," we say. To me, this means keep coming back to the Healer *and* the meetings. The daily, ongoing nature of our healing is the simple truth of our new existence. Simple but not easy.

A failure to acknowledge our need for healing can result in people who "go to church" their whole lives but never become Christians. We never come to terms with our own woundedness. We never see the severity of the thorn in our flesh. We can see quite obviously the thorn in the flesh of others, just not in our own. We say, "Well, I've never been to jail, jammed a needle in my arm, or exchanged sex for drugs behind a dumpster," and we convince ourselves that our particular thorn is not that bad.

However, if this were true, the church would not be seen as a hypocritical, judgmental community of harm rather than a place of healing. In *Fresh Expressions in a Digital Age*, I argued that the church must become a place of healing again.[1] I'm not referring to faith healers doing miracles on stages, televised and monetized. I often find one aspect of my ministry is cleaning up the mess after that circus, and grieving alongside the people harmed by it. The church should be a place where wounded people can come and be made well again, not with flashy miracles, but by finding a safe place where they can unbandage and bare their wounds in a community of love and forgiveness.

〰〰〰〰〰

Healing is long, slow, gradual work.

This is what Pastor Dan was trying to tell me when I went from eighteen-year-old drug-dealing, gang-leading felon to preacher overnight: "Jesus will save your soul, but AA will save your ass." As real and powerful as my encounter with Christ was, it did not "cure" me. It set me on a lifelong journey of healing, a journey we all have to make for ourselves.

I have pastored several churches throughout my ministry, but none of them have been the place where I experienced the kind of community that Jesus intended. When I want to go to "church," I go to a recovery group.

Every week, I meet in church basements and classrooms with folks from various religious beliefs, and we have *church*. Most are not Christians and would never darken a sanctuary door on Sunday. But many spend more time at the church than longtime members do. They gather for the same reasons as the Sunday morning crowd. They long to know God, they desire the fellowship of other human beings, and they want to learn how to pray and meditate. While some just want to stay sober, they discover that to do that they have to pursue a relationship with God.

While my friends in these anonymous fellowships may not proclaim faith in Jesus Christ, the Holy Spirit is active and alive in them and empowering them to live a different kind of life—one free of drugs and alcohol. In fact, well-meaning churches and ministries can inoculate people with the "Jesus cure" just enough that they never actually find true recovery. Jesus is not confined to church sanctuaries. He is also found in basements, club houses, and classrooms where recovering people huddle around their coffee pots.

They don't have to know Jesus' name for Jesus to know their names.

The crazy Methodist tribe to which I belong believes in a radical phenomenon called *prevenient grace*, which simply means, "the grace that goes before us." Before we are aware, before we want to reciprocate, before we believe—God is after us. God is wooing us, pursuing us, calling out, "Where are you?" We can only "love because God first loved us" (1 John 4:19). Our healing is a response to God's love, initiated, completed, and sustained by God alone.

God is drawing all humanity into a relationship in this way. We are sent with hearts aflame with God's love to give our lives to God's grand search-and-recovery effort. But we need to know that God is working in the people already before we get there.

It is inappropriate to refer to 12-step fellowships as "secular" programs. There are fewer places in the world more sacred. God is incredibly active in the rooms of recovery fellowships. When I need healing, when I need to experience God's grace, when I need to see other people experiencing "redemption," when I need to go to *church*, the kind envisioned and built by Jesus, I go to the "rooms."

I am ordained clergy, but I was not "discipled" by the United Methodist Church. I went through decades of training and education, but no one ever took me aside and said, "Let me teach you how to follow Jesus . . . Follow me." I was discipled by Alcoholics Anonymous, which is a gift that few lifelong churchgoers ever have the joy of receiving.

In the *Big Book of Alcoholics Anonymous*, it says that we have been given "a design for living."[2] If this sounds similar to daily manna in the wilderness, power made perfect in weakness, and "don't worry about tomorrow because each day has enough trouble," that's because it is.

The architects of the Twelve Steps, Bill W. and Dr. Bob, were both Christians. When they met in 1935, the Oxford Group was responsible for bringing them together. They didn't invent the Twelve Steps. Rather, they adapted and codified most of its tenets into the AA program. The Oxford Group, initially called "First Century Christian Fellowship" at its formation in 1921, was the brainchild of Lutheran priest Frank Buchman. For Buchman, fear and selfishness were the cause of human suffering. Buchman was resolved that the only solution to the human condition was to "surrender one's life over to God's plan."

Bill and Bob employed many of the foundational tenets of the Oxford Group to build a program focused specifically on the problem of alcoholism. Consider these words, some of the precedents of the now widely known key ideas, language, and structure of AA:

> You cannot belong to the Oxford Group. It has no membership list, subscriptions, badge, rules, or definite location. It is a name for a group of people who, from every rank, profession, and trade, in many countries, have surrendered their lives to God and who are endeavouring to lead a spiritual quality of life under the guidance the Holy Spirit.

> The Oxford Group is not a religion; it has no hierarchy, no temples, no endowments; Its workers have no salaries, no plans but God's Plan; every country is their country, every man their brother.[3]

The Oxford Group is not a religion; it has no hierarchy, no temples, no The Oxford Group has four points that are the keys to the kind of spiritual life God wishes us to lead. These points are:

1. Absolute Honesty.

2. Absolute Purity.

3. Absolute Unselfishness.

4. Absolute Love.

The Oxford Group four points are the basis of beauty of thought, word, and deed. They may not be so unattainable as we may suppose, but very few can or have ever lived lives of Absolute Honesty, Purity, Unselfishness, and Love. "For all have sinned and come short of the glory of God", St. Paul tells us.[4]

A similar version of this language is preserved in the AA literature and group readings to this day. It is a widely held misunderstanding that the Oxford Group had "six steps." In actuality, the group held four practical spiritual activities that were adopted and rephrased by AA.

To be spiritually reborn and to live in the state in which these four points are the guides to our life in God, the Oxford Group advocate four practical spiritual activities:

1. The Sharing of our sins and temptations with another Christian life given to God, and to use Sharing as Witness to help others, still unchanged, to recognize and acknowledge their sins.

2. Surrender of our life, past, present, and future, into God's keeping and direction.

3. Restitution to all whom we have wronged directly or indirectly.

4. Listening to, accepting, relying on God's Guidance and carrying it out in everything we do or say, great or small.

These spiritual activities have proved indispensable to countless numbers who are living changed lives. They are not new ideas nor inventions of the Oxford Group. They are the tenets of simple Christianity.[5]

Jesus teaches us in the Sermon on the Mount that our design for living begins with understanding that to be "poor in spirit" is to be blessed. It's not those who make their way by their own power and ingenuity who are blessed; rather, "blessed are the meek," for they will "inherit the earth" (Matt 5:1-3, 5). Meekness is not weakness. It is "strength under control." Jesus is meekness embodied. The one in whom the fullness of God was pleased to dwell emptied himself by taking the form of a servant (Col 1:19; Phil 2:6–7).

The journey starts by admitting our poverty of spirit. We acknowledge that we need God to manage our lives and that we come to God in a state of brokenness, infected with indwelling sin (Rom 7:18). Only from that position—that is, from our knees—can we enter rightly into a relationship with God. We come to the end of ourselves, and we come to believe (see Luke 15:17).

The first move of the spiritual life is captured by the word repentance (Gk. μετάνοια: *metanoia*). Jesus arrives at the scene of our souls proclaiming not, "Hey, you're doing great; keep it up!" But rather "Repent and believe!" This indicates turning 180 degrees the other direction; it requires an entire "psychic change,"[6] a new mind, and a restored soul.

Many Christians stop here, but in the words of TV product evangelists, "Wait . . . There's more!" In a place of surrender, we make a decision to turn our lives and our wills over to God's care. Jesus is not only Savior; Jesus is Lord. In view of God's mercy, we take seriously Paul's encouragement to "offer your bodies as a living sacrifice, holy and pleasing to God—this is your true and proper worship" (Rom 12:1).

Some Christians make it this far in the design—"But wait! There's more!" We then have to do an inventory of our souls (Lam 3:40) and confess "[our] sins to each other and pray for each other so that you may be healed" (James 5:16). God's healing and transforming grace gives us the power to actually change. We ask God to remove our defects and empower us to live differently (James 4:10). Power made perfect in weakness includes not only forgiveness, but becoming a "new creation" (2 Cor 5:17).

Very few Christians make it to the next leg of the journey of grace, where we must now go back and *right all our wrongs*. We must offer reparation and healing for the harm we've caused to others. Jesus tells us, "If you are offering your gift at the altar and there remember that your brother has something against you, leave your gift there in front of the altar. First go and be reconciled to them; then come and offer your gift" (Matt 5:23–24).

Finally, we continue to live out this design for the rest of our lives. We grow in our relationship with God though prayer, meditation, and other spiritual disciplines. Jesus teaches us the key here is in "abiding." Abiding is about remaining, dwelling, and staying connected to Jesus, like a branch that depends on a vine for life. *Abiding* in Christ is something we never complete or graduate, and at some point, being a branch on the vine leads to bearing fruit, "fruit that will last" (see John 15:1–8).

Bearing fruit is an expectation of the spiritual life, but this is much more about *being* than *doing*. Abiding is not about making things happen in our own strength, it's about watching for what God is already up to and joining in. It is not about effort, but rather receiving a gift. Yet it is a gift we cannot keep to ourselves; we have to give it away to keep it. When doing flows from our being, we become a community of wounded healers, sharing the gift of healing grace with others, carrying the message in our daily lives to the ends of the earth (Acts 1:8).

The six steps developed by early AA members before the *Big Book* may sound familiar:

1. A Complete deflation.

2. Dependence on God.

3. A Moral inventory.

4. Confession.

5. Restitution.

6. Continued work with others in need.

The Twelve Steps as we have them today were developed in the process of writing the *Big Book* in late 1938, as an expansion of the six steps. Part of the effectiveness of 12-step recovery fellowships lies in distilling the journey of salvation (i.e., healing) into a journey of steps that are clear, succinct, and attainable for most people.

The steps facilitate the three movements of Nouwen's *Reaching Out*, to ourselves, to others, and to a higher power. The "design for living" encapsulated in the Twelve Steps is a playbook for becoming a person who embodies the life of Jesus. The steps read as follows:

1. We admitted we were powerless over alcohol [or whatever sin or addiction]—that our lives had become unmanageable.

2. Came to believe that a Power greater than ourselves could restore us to sanity.

3. Made a decision to turn our will and our lives over to the care of God as *we understood Him.*

4. Made a searching and fearless moral inventory of ourselves.

5. Admitted to God, to ourselves, and to another human being the exact nature of our wrongs.

6. Were entirely ready to have God remove all these defects of character.

7. Humbly asked Him to remove our shortcomings.

8. Made a list of all persons we had harmed, and became willing to make amends to them all.

9. Made direct amends to such people wherever possible, except when to do so would injure them or others.

10. Continued to take personal inventory and when we were wrong promptly admitted it.

11. Sought through prayer and meditation to improve our conscious contact with God *as we understood Him*, praying only for knowledge of His will for us and the power to carry that out.

12. Having had a spiritual awakening as the result of these steps, we tried to carry this message to alcoholics, and to practice these principles in all our affairs.[7]

The parallels between the steps and the teaching of Jesus are not accidental. Catholic theologian and healer Father Richard Rohr emphasized the connection between the *Big Book of Alcoholics Anonymous* and the Gospel in *Breathing Under Water: Spirituality and the Twelve Steps*. Rohr believes the Twelve Steps of Alcoholics Anonymous are America's most significant and authentic contribution to the history of spirituality. He sees the steps as an accessible version of the Christian faith, which provides a manageable design for life in a broken society.

Rick Warren and John Baker of Saddleback Church in a sense reclaimed the Twelve Steps for Christianity in their now global program Celebrate Recovery (CR). They expanded the steps to again include all forms of human woundedness: hurts, habits, and hangups. Hurts cover past physical, sexual, or emotional abuse and family dysfunction (i.e., wounds). Habits refer to addictions, such as drugs, alcohol, sex, gambling, food, or anything else we idolize. Hang-ups refer to negative mental attitudes, like anxiety, depression, or low self-esteem. Essentially, it means anything that causes shame, guilt, despair, depression, anger, or pain.

CR helps us acknowledge that every human being is in recovery from sin. We all have lost our Garden of Eden. We all have known the gift of desperation in some way. Not all of us suffer from the diseases that show up as addictions, but each of us has a broken condition that manifests in the various ways we try to fill the hole in our being with the temporary balms of food, sex, work, control, approval, and other banes.

The steps are not a series of boxes to be checked, after which one is suddenly "cured." One does not graduate this program. These steps are a lifelong journey of spiritual growth. They keep us in touch with our "thorns" and give us a way to remain in communion with our wounded healer. The "design" is a process of yielding our weaknesses to God, where we find the perfect power of grace.

The steps are our lived response to Jesus' question, "Do you want to be well?"

Shortly after I was released from my final incarceration, I heard of a United Methodist pastor named Jorge Acevedo. Jorge also comes from a background of addiction. Born on February 1, 1960, in Santurce, Puerto Rico, Jorge is a self-described "military brat." His father was a tech sergeant in the United States Air Force. His mother was a classroom teacher for thirty-two years who worked mostly with disadvantaged children in poverty-stricken communities. Her work planted the seeds of his desire to be in ministry with "the ones no one else wants or sees."

Jorge lived at Air Force bases in Charleston, South Carolina; San Bernardino, California; and Puerto Rico, before returning to Charleston. His family finally settled in Orlando, Florida, when he began junior high school in 1972. Jorge's father was a workaholic, driven to lift his family out of poverty. He also struggled with alcoholism, as did his father before him.

Jorge's family was nominally Roman Catholic, and Jorge served as an altar boy as a child. One priest in particular nurtured and fascinated him, planting the seed for serving as a minister in his heart. But the family connection to church waned for Jorge in junior high. Jorge had his first drunk episode at twelve years old. His interest in drugs and alcohol increased through age seventeen. While more of a "situational" abuser of drugs and alcohol, when life was tough, he would use to excess. The harder adolescent life got as he perceived it, the more dependent he became on substances.

By Jorge's senior year of high school, he was abusing drugs, alcohol, and sex. One day, an area Campus Crusade for Christ director came into his life. Ultimately, through his nurturing and influence, Jorge decided to give his life to Christ. He and his friends celebrated his conversion by smoking a joint. Obviously, Jorge was not fully aware of the magnitude of his decision, yet the prevenient grace of God was at work in his life. Jorge found a home and became the summer youth intern at Pine Castle United Methodist Church, where a charismatic preacher invested in him as a young disciple.

While sitting in the top row of a physics class at Valencia Community College, studying to be an architect, a question shot through his brain. "What brings you joy?" the Voice asked.

Jorge responded, "Helping teach the junior high school Sunday class."

Something burst inside of Jorge in that moment. He stood up, gathered his books, and walked out of the classroom, never to return. Ultimately, he went to Asbury Theological Seminary, became an ordained elder, and has served at one of the largest, most successful congregations in Methodism for twenty-six years, Grace Church in southwest Florida.

What impressed me about Jorge was his complete transparency about his struggles. He actually used his brokenness to build Grace Church, which has had one of the strongest Celebrate Recovery programs in the nation for two decades. Recently they created their own contextually faithful variation, called Choose Recovery.

In my first year of sobriety, fresh out of jail, hearing about Jorge and then connecting to him changed the trajectory of my life. Pastors could be ex–drug addicts and not only find healing but make their recovery an integral part of their ministry? I knew other clergy who were in recovery, but they didn't talk about it openly to their congregations. Jorge was different; he was painting with ashes.

Over the years Jorge has become one of my closest mentors. He's shown me that having a "thorn in the flesh" is a gift, not a curse. God's power truly is made perfect in our weaknesses. He has embodied God's "design for living" in a way that I and many others could learn to follow.

10

LEARNING BACK TO LIFE

Happy are those who find wisdom,
and those who get understanding.

Proverbs 3:13 NRSV

Catherine Mumford was born on January 17, 1829, in Ashbourne, Derbyshire, England, to staunch Methodist parents who were active in the temperance movement. She was the only daughter of five children. Unfortunately, of her four brothers, John, the youngest, was the only one to survive infancy. Her father, an entrepreneur, founded a coach-building business. Her mother taught her from home. Despite her limited access to formal education, by the age of five she could read, and by twelve she had completed her eighth reading of the entire Bible.[1]

In 1841, when Catherine was twelve, her mother was persuaded to send her to school. But her brief time in the classroom was cut short by a serious curvature of the spine. Her condition left her lying facedown in a makeshift hammock for months. She was never able to return to school, but this didn't stop her from teaching herself. She began voraciously to study church history and theology. She devoured the writings of John Wesley and John Fletcher. She dove into the works of the Lutheran historians Johann Lorenz Mosheim and Augustus Neander, as well as the American revivalist Charles Finney. She read Joseph Butler's *Analogy of Religion*, Isaac Newton's writings on prophecy, and John Bunyan's *The Pilgrim's Progress*.[2] Her central fascination became the first centuries of Christianity and the teachings and problems of the early church.

In 1844 her father, once a champion of the temperance movement, relapsed into alcoholism. His business fell into shambles. This along with Catherine's own struggles with the symptoms and side effects of scoliosis, wounded her adolescent years. Yet, she continued to read, study, and learn.

On the morning of June 15, 1846, she joyfully shared her conversion with her mother. The familiar words of her hymn book came alive: "My God I am Thine! What a comfort Divine, What a blessing to know that my Jesus is mine!" While this conversion launched her into a soul struggle to pursue sanctification, she lived in fear of backsliding into sin.[3]

Catherine's longing for the reformation of Methodism was awakened during this time. Shortly after John Wesley's death in 1791, Methodism had begun to splinter into various factions. Many believed the Methodist movement had become domesticated, losing its evangelical fervor and missional focus, existing "as a dead sect, having the form of religion without the power." Various groups represented a movement to reform Methodism. One group broke away as early as 1797 to form the Methodist New Connexion.

Catherine's outspoken support of the reform movement resulted in the nonrenewal of her quarterly Wesleyan Methodist membership ticket. This left her a kind of spiritual orphan for a time. Additionally, throughout the years of 1848–51, abiding physical pain from both scoliosis and tuberculosis accompanied her spiritual anguish.[4]

None of these adversities, however, were able to stop Catherine Mumford, whom the world would later know as Catherine Booth, cofounder of the Salvation Army.

After her marriage to William Booth on June 16, 1855, Catherine struggled with a stirring that she felt was a call to a public ministry of preaching and teaching. The couple had found a short-lived ministry in the New Methodist Connexion. There she took her first timid steps into her call to public ministry, leading a class meeting, teaching senior girls Sunday school, and giving temperance lectures. In May 1858 William was ordained as a minister at the New Connexion's annual conference and appointed to Gateshead, where once his requests to evangelistic work were denied, as a superintendent minister.

Walking among the poverty-stricken streets one Sunday evening, Catherine felt a strong compulsion to stop and speak to the women in the dilapidated homes rather than go to the chapel for the service. One woman she encountered was carrying a jug of beer to her alcoholic husband who was bedridden due to his drunken condition. Catherine went to their home, listened intently to their story, then shared the parable of the prodigal son. The encounter left them all in tears. After Catherine led the couple in a time of prayer, she felt a new resolve to begin an evangelistic ministry of visitation, prayer, and practical help.[5]

Catherine was inspired by American holiness revivalist Phoebe Palmer, whose public preaching ministry was bringing hundreds of people to Christ. Phoebe's ministry, however, also attracted powerful critics, who rose up to condemn both revivalism and women's right to preach. This led Catherine, who was yet to speak publicly, to publish her first pamphlet defending the principle of female ministry. Catherine's compelling argument was constructed from a range of Old and New Testament texts. Her essays engaged leading modern and ancient scholars and contained detailed exegeses of scriptural passages that supposedly prohibited female ministry.

Shortly after this, Catherine Booth stepped forward to break her silence and began to speak publicly. She quickly became a celebrity. She spoke to large crowds and was unable to accept the many invitations that poured in. When William became sick, she not only fulfilled his preaching responsibilities but managed the circuit affairs. William ultimately resigned from the Methodist New Connexion, and the Booths became key figures in the Second Evangelical Awakening. Catherine became the prime apologist for the movement, not only addressing large crowds, but securing finances, attaining buildings, and organizing the system.

The hammock-ridden daughter of an alcoholic with no access to higher education became known as the intellectual and theological brainchild of the Salvation Army.

Tragically, Catherine became sick with an aggressive form of breast cancer and deteriorated rapidly. She preached her last sermon on June 21, 1888, at the City Temple in Holborn. She helped prepare the final drafts of *Darkest England*, and floods of faithful visitors came on pilgrimage to visit her sickbed, a kind of altar to her faithfulness to Christ. At her death, the growing army of Salvationists were already scattered across the globe.

She died on Saturday October 4, 1890, and her body was taken to the Army's Clapton Congress Hall. An estimated fifty thousand people came to her lying in state. Thousands more attended her funeral services, and the *Methodist Times* described Catherine as the Army's "inspiring soul" and "restraining genius."[6]

Catherine Booth is the mother of Salvation Army theology. From her mind, heart, and soul, the movement of Salvationism was unleashed on the world. It is a movement that has touched millions of lives, brought ministry to the darkest places, and encouraged the acceptance of women in ministry.

Catherine Booth painted with ashes, and the world was her canvas. Her passion to learn and educate others has been an inspiration to many.

＊＊＊＊＊

Decades later, another young lady with a passion for peace, education, and the right for girls to attend school was born in the Swat Valley of Pakistan. She was actively campaigning for equal access to education in the face of tremendous danger to her own life. She had even begun to attain financial awards for her campaigning. Journalists and foreigners were coming to visit. The Taliban was none too pleased with these activities. In her words, they "want to hide us [girls] away."

On Tuesday, October 9, 2012, Malala Yousafzai was riding the bus to school when a group of men with firearms obstructed the road and pulled the bus over. She remembered one of the men saying, "Who is Malala?" When the other students looked in her direction, the man pulled out a black Colt 45 and fired three shots. The first bullet went through her left eye socket and came out under her left shoulder. She slumped over onto her friend, blood pouring from her left ear, and the other two bullets hit the girls next to her.[7]

The attacker's bullet would not stop this young Pakistani activist for female education. She became the youngest ever Nobel Prize laureate. Her advocacy for human rights, particularly the education of women and children, has grown into an international movement. In her native Swat Valley in Khyber Pakhtunkhwa, northwest Pakistan, the local Pakistani Taliban had banned girls from attending school. What her attackers meant for ill placed her on the world's stage, which she used as a force for massive good. Millions of girls have been helped by her work, and she is now widely considered the most prominent citizen in her country.

For me, these two brave women are champions for the values of equality and education. They understood that learning is inextricably linked to living, and they were willing to put their lives on the line to embody those values.

Most Americans take education for granted. We also falsely assume that all people have equal access and opportunity. When the possibility of education is removed, or obstructed, we realize what a gift it is.

My own limited access to education was a problem mostly of my own making. Nevertheless, the halls of academia were not a warm place for a ninth-grade drop out. When I finally stopped running from my call, it became abundantly clear that extensive schooling would be a necessary component of what came next. I didn't have much hope that I could actually get through the required education, but with the encouragement of my mentors, I decided to go to college and pursue a degree.

I had taken my GED exam as a teenager in a state institute for incarcerated juvenile felons. Somehow, I miraculously aced it, even though I was missing three years of high school education. Regardless, I had to begin anew in the educational process. I was ill-equipped for higher learning and was at a tremendous disadvantage. When I enrolled in college, I couldn't understand half the words the professors spoke, so I purchased a pocket dictionary, wrote them down, and looked them up later.

As a child, I couldn't hold my pencil correctly. I clenched my fist to operate the writing instrument. The teachers assumed I was mentally handicapped. They provided me triangle pencil grips to try and train my hand, but I just slid them to the top and wrote in a way comfortable to me. This made me the brunt of many jokes. Later they discovered I was just ambidextrous. Sitting in class as a first-semester college student, I decided I would not be the object of ridicule from fellow classmates. I trained my hands how to hold a pencil correctly in the process of taking notes.

Additionally, I am mathematically challenged. I took three preparatory math classes just to get up to speed for a course in basic algebra. Countless hours of practice problems with Mozart, Vivaldi, and John Barry movie scores playing in the background helped me along. I am deeply indebted to those first professors. I was in their offices day and night with a barrage of questions. They were very patient with me and quickly found a way to put me to good use grading and proofreading papers.

Learning the lingo of higher education was like learning a new language for me. Yet, it became apparent that by the grace of God I had not burned up all my brain cells.

My strategy was simple. I took up residence in the library. I would arrange my schedule to take an early morning class and an evening class. When the morning class was finished, I would inhabit my favorite quiet corner of the library. There I would read, study, and write until it was time for the evening class. I maintained that practice while working multiple jobs and running a startup company. I discovered that the same drive that had helped me survive the streets could be applied in a positive way toward pursuing an education.

I was soon making straight As. I received an invitation to join Phi Theta Kappa international honor society and eventually became the chair of the tutoring committee for that organization. I spent hours giving back to other students what had been freely given to me.

I was chosen as the male representative for the PTK annual conference for our chapter and flown to Nashville, Tennessee. It was the first time I'd left Florida since I was a child. I found myself suddenly eligible for merit-based scholarships and made my way to the dean's list every semester of my education. My poetry was published in *Imprints*, the college magazine, two years in a row. I was inducted into the Community of Scholars honors program, which paid for every honors class I had taken. I had a newfound love for this educational journey.

Through my education, I was *learning back to life*. I found meaning and purpose. I decided I was not worthless. I realized that God could use even me.

I worked my way through the College of Central Florida and then Saint Leo University. I prayed before every test, and prayerfully submitted every assignment. While I was not naturally more intelligent than my colleagues, it seemed I brought a different work ethic to our studies. Maybe feeling as though I didn't really deserve to be there fueled my drive. Ultimately, I graduated with highest honors from Saint Leo University with a BA in psychology.

My next stop was the Orlando campus of Asbury Theological Seminary. One glaring problem was that I couldn't afford to go, and I was trying to practice a no-debt policy. I wrote a letter to the president of the seminary, sharing my story, and that I felt God had called me to attend there. I didn't have high hopes for a response, but to my surprise the president responded and brought me before his board to share my journey. People on that board began to step forward and commit personally to fund my education.

At Asbury, I employed the same approach of taking up residence as a library hermit. Through the generosity of those private donors and merit-based scholarships, I was able to graduate with highest honors, debt-free. I was awarded the Zondervan Greek Scholarship Award, also known by my wife as the "Bible Nerd Award." Each year, the seminary gave an award called the Towel and Basin to one graduating senior who was selected by the student body and faculty. The award is given to the graduate who most embodies the life and ministry of Jesus. It is the most prestigious award given by Asbury. My colleagues and professors selected me as the recipient for my graduating class.

The Towel and Basin award is a bronze statue of Jesus down on his knees, washing the feet of a disciple. It sits on my desk now as I write these words. It is a daily reminder that Jesus is calling me to join him in the work of washing feet.

After a yearlong break from graduating with a 96-credit hour master of divinity, I longed for the classroom again. Through a miraculous turn of events, I found myself studying under one of my mentors, Dr. Leonard Sweet at George Fox University. I earned a doctor of ministry in semiotics and future studies. I wrote three full dissertations, one a year for three years. Every time I finished a dissertation it was modified and published as a book. So, I decided as long as publishers were willing, I would keep writing.

My final dissertation, on contextual intelligence, was published with my mentor and now coauthor Dr. Sweet. Shortly after graduation, I began helping him with a few classes, and an opportunity opened up to come aboard at United Theological Seminary in Dayton, Ohio, as an adjunct professor. Later I was named the director of the Fresh Expressions House of Studies. Now I design courses and teach doctoral, master's, and certificate-level classes. I mentor the most amazing group of doctoral students, each one of them a world changer.

There are few places in the world I am more comfortable than in a classroom. I have become a lifelong learner, and one of the roles I greatly enjoy is teaching. The most important thing I can say about my educational journey is that it continues today. Twelve years as a student in higher education taught me how to learn. Now, as I shepherd doctoral students through their educational journey, I stay on the cutting edge of front-line learning.

Education is not merely a process for me; it is redemptive. Jesus created a community of "learners," which is the English translation of the Greek word (*mathétés*), or "disciple."

To stop learning is in some ways to stop living and to stop following Jesus.

The lives of Catherine Booth and Malala Yousafzai show us that against all circumstances, a will to learn, the courage to write and speak, and a heart to heal the wounded can unleash movements of grace that transfigure the world. Unfortunately, the very thing that those caught in a lifestyle of addiction and criminality need—education—is often inaccessible.

I wasn't always teaching doctoral cohorts. My very first students were quite literally a captive audience. Shortly after my final release, I returned to the Marion County Jail, where I'd once resided—through the front door this time. The jail has been one of my most consistent classrooms over the years. I began teaching students under the umbrella of a program called Christian 12 Step (C12).

During that final incarceration, I received the Christian 12 Step book and began to read, work the steps, and go to meetings. Christian 12 Step is an organization that encourages inner healing through Christ to overcome dependencies and emotional struggles. They send free study guides in both English and Spanish to inmates in jails and prisons to all fifty states and several foreign countries. At this time, inmates from more than nine hundred correctional institutions have either received the study guide or have enrolled in the Student Correspondence Course. Currently, C12 sends approximately four hundred books into jails and prisons to incarcerated men and women every month. Additionally, C12 groups gather in churches throughout the country.

The day I was released and our only vehicle broke down, a friend from C12 picked me up and got me to a meeting. Soon I became friends with Lonnie Earnest, the executive director of this international ministry. Lonnie was once a pastor of one of the most thriving Southern Baptist congregations in the country. He fell into sexual sin, lost his church, and was sent to prison. When he was released, he began to serve Jesus in a different way. As the director of Christian 12 Step for the last twenty years, he has impacted the lives of millions of people across the world and disciples a small army of young Christian leaders. Lonnie became my mentor and spiritual father. I call him "Dad" to this day.

Going back into the same jail where I used to reside as an inmate to teach others about Jesus was an integral part of my early recovery.

In my class, we spent some of our time learning about the Bible, but also many other countless subjects.

It was through teaching in the jail that I met my youngest daughter for the first time. My sponsor taught me that the "wherever possible" part of the ninth step is God's part. So, as we make "direct amends to such people wherever possible, except when to do so would injure them or others," we know there are "wild cards." There are things we can't make right, and things we don't know. Some amends are "living amends" when making them would do more harm than good. In my case, I knew that there was a possibility of more children out there.

One day, walking into the Marion County Jail to teach my students, God did God's part. As I was crossing through the visitation area, a little eighteen-month-old girl running for the candy machine slammed into my leg. I looked down into her eyes and had a strange moment of recognition. An older couple stopped me, read my instructor badge, and said, "You're Michael Beck? That little girl is your daughter, Angel." They were there visiting their daughter, who was currently incarcerated, one of the women I had slept with in my days of drugs and sex.

This created quite a mess, particularly with my soon-to-be bride, Jill Beck. I called my sponsor, and he walked me though the process of making amends. I immediately took responsibility for Angel and was granted full custody. Jill, initially furious that our family had grown from seven to eight children in one chance meeting, took Angel in and nurtured her as her own. Jill says, "Some of my kids were born from my womb. Angel was born from my heart." Angel's biological mother, who struggled with addiction her entire life, tragically died without Angel ever getting to meet her. Although I wasn't given a chance to name Angel Joy Beck, her name is quite appropriate. She is truly an angel and brings joy to every life she touches.

What is the probability of this chance encounter at the local jailhouse? Angels in green suits, actions done in ill that are used for good, being maneuvered through the messiness right into the place you are supposed to be, and God was right in the middle of it all.

Angel wasn't the only child that the jail gifted to me. There would be many more in the coming years. Florida has one of the largest prison populations in the United States and is one of the leaders in the privatization of prisons. "Direct-file" juveniles are housed until they turn eighteen and then sentenced as adults, even if they committed their crimes at twelve or thirteen years old. Some of the youth who committed the most severe offenses were housed in a special unit in the adult jail. If you've read about youth committing murders, armed robberies, rapes, and major drug crimes, they have passed through my classroom. Eventually I became the primary teacher to these young students and one of the only adults they saw on a weekly basis. Many have no hope of ever being released. Under current sentencing guidelines, they will spend their lives incarcerated.

My life experience makes me uniquely qualified to love and invest in them. While working with them rarely achieves a change in their court cases, I often see a massive change in their souls. Liberation doesn't always have to do with tangible freedom. However, for those fortunate enough to be given another chance, I mentor and walk beside them. Through that mentoring relationship, I pass on what was given to me.

Oftentimes, these young people need to be taught basic skills they didn't receive from an absentee father. One of my greatest joys occurs when I take my wife out to dinner, and a former student comes up and tells us he or she is clean, has a job, and is staying out of trouble. Several of them have joined our church and become influencers over the years.

While it is frustrating at times that all our best efforts have little effect on the system as a whole, nevertheless, a huge kingdom impact is made when one life is changed (Luke 15:7).

One essential piece of God's identity—God acts to redeem Israel from bondage. "Liberation is the activity of God."[8] This God comes into history and liberates humans from an enslaved condition (Exod 6:6–7; 20:1; Deut 24:18), thus revealing God's defining essence throughout the Old Testament as חֶסֶד (*checed*), "mercy" or "unfailing love" (Exod 34:6–7).

This liberating God puts on flesh in the incarnation of Jesus Christ. Jesus demonstrates solidarity with the poor and the oppressed, topples empires through nonviolent resistance, and liberates all humanity from an enslaved condition (Luke 1:52–55). Furthermore, Jesus said that peacemakers will be called "children of God" (Matt 5:9). God the Spirit infills and equips the church to continue Jesus' "peacemaking" activities in a world where war, systemic injustice, unequal access to education, and corruption at every level of government thrive.

As the church, we are called to be a community that advocates for justice, education, freedom, equality, and peace for all God's children. By the power of the Holy Spirit, the church must labor against injustice, witnessing to God's present and future reign of peace. Christians have a rich history of contending for vulnerable populations, including the poor, the marginalized, the immigrant, the abused, and the neglected.

Methodism founder John Wesley reminds us that personal holiness must eventually be expressed through social holiness. Holiness is something that is lived out in the real world among our fellow human beings, not something that is enshrined between the walls of a church or a monastery.

The communities where I live and serve are torn apart by drugs, delinquency, homelessness, unemployment, and domestic violence. Addiction in some way has touched every incarcerated prisoner, every battered woman, every homeless family, and every neglected/abused child. While addiction touches every social class, it particularly manifests unjustly in the lives of the poor. Desperate people do desperate things. My own life is a witness to this injustice.

One of the greatest injustices I labor subversively against is the United States justice system itself, which is little more than a modern form of slavery. I have stood with my young, incarcerated students as they were sentenced. I have come before the judge to offer a report of their changed lives and of their progress inside. I've watched black and brown youth receive twenty-year sentences for crimes committed by white counterparts who went home on probation. I've seen firsthand the disparity in sentencing between someone who can afford legal representation and someone dependent on the services of a public defender.

I grew up in a multiethnic neighborhood on the edge of the projects. We read about segregation as part of history, but it was not our direct experience. My best friend and several longtime girlfriends were persons of color. We lived together, got high together, broke the law together, and got locked up together. We were a kind of big, dysfunctional street family. But our bonds were thick and real. Incarceration culture encourages groups that form around race, so I was considered a race traitor.

The justice system itself preserves the legacy of systemic oppression that Martin Luther King Jr. fought against. The goal is not reformation but rather punishment. The experience of black or brown persons regarding sentencing, treatment, and supposed rehabilitation are not equal to their white counterparts'. Because of white privilege and the ability to afford an attorney, my outcome was different. I have seen this again and again in the outcomes of my students.

The prison system rarely reforms anyone. It mostly creates better criminals.

Recidivism is defined as the relapse of criminal behavior that results in the rearrest, reconviction, and reimprisonment of an individual after initial incarceration. The US has one of the highest recidivism rates in the world. A 2019 study showed that 83 percent of state prisoners reoffended within nine years, 45 percent within the first year of release.[9] Persons of color disproportionately make up the prison population and receive harsher sentences. While many social justice groups have sought to change this reality, the church remains largely silent. While the problem as a whole seems overwhelming, each of us can take an active role in working with those in our immediate relational sphere to bring grassroots change.

In my experience the key for those caught in the system to become productive citizens is threefold: a spiritual awakening, a supportive community, and access to education.

Being released onto the streets homeless with seven kids and a broken-down vehicle did not play in my favor. There were times I considered going back to old, illegal entrepreneurial ventures. The difference for me was the miraculous intervention of God, a loving church community, the recovery fellowship, and access to an education. I went from the school of hard knocks to the halls of academia.

Perhaps in some way, all wounded healers are living to learn and learning to live. But we must be aware that all people are not provided equal access to learning. If the church would take an active role in prison and education reform, we would more effectively create communities of healing—and have a lot more people painting with ashes.

11

ONLY AS SICK
AS OUR SECRETS

*Therefore, confess your sins to one another, and pray for one
another, so that you may be healed. The prayer of the righteous
is powerful and effective.*

James 5:16 NRSV

What began with a simple act of theft, stealing fruit, happened not
because he was hungry but because it was forbidden. This kind of
behavior was beginning to take a darker turn for the boy named
Augustine. As he transitioned from childhood into adolescence, he
fell into the darkness of lust. Under the pressure of his friends, who
boasted of their string of sexual exploits, he began experimentations
of his own. He became obsessed with the opposite sex and was de-
veloping a compulsion to act out sexually. Once his father discovered
his sexual exploits, rather than condemning him, he celebrated the
potential for grandchildren that would soon be following his son's
conquests.

His mother, however, was none too pleased with her son's de-
scent into the darkness of lust. She warned strongly that his behavior
would lead to destruction and even death. The struggle between his
sexual compulsions and his desire to be a good person intensified.

Around the age of seventeen, Augustine began a love affair with
a concubine that would last more than fifteen years. He broke off the
relationship when his mother arranged a marriage to a ten-year-old
heiress from a respectable family, which was the common practice in

his day. However, this wedding was not possible for two more years. He had to wait for her to reach the legal age of twelve. During this waiting period, he procured another concubine to satiate his sexual desires.

It was during this in-between period, in late August of the year 386, that Augustine heard the mysterious voice of a child nearby say, "Take up and read." He randomly opened a book of Saint Paul's writings and read Romans 13:13–14: "Let us live honorably as in the day, not in reveling and drunkenness, not in debauchery and licentiousness, not in quarreling and jealousy. Instead, put on the Lord Jesus Christ, and make no provision for the flesh, to gratify its desires" (NRSV). This led him to a place of deep penitence and confession of his sins. He broke off his engagement to his eleven-year-old fiancée, left the relationships with his two concubines behind, and became a priest.

We know him today as Saint Augustine, one of the most influential theologians, philosophers, and writers in Western Christianity. Ultimately, he would become the bishop of Hippo Regius in Numidia, Roman North Africa. As measured by surviving works, he was among the most prolific Latin authors, with more than one hundred separate titles attributed to him. Many scholars argue that no Christian beside Saint Paul has more shaped the church of the West as we know it, and the fields of philosophy and ethics.

Perhaps his most notable work was a thirteen-book confession of his early struggles and his conversion experience, written while he was in his early forties. *Confessions* became one of the great classics of Christian theology and the first Christian autobiography ever written. Augustine weaved into this account of his own life an outpouring of penitence and theological reflection. By retracing the steps of his life, he also reflected on evil, original sin, incarnation, the fully human fully divine nature of Christ, time, eternity, resurrection, and eschatology.

Saint Augustine used the confession of his own brokenness, the movement from sin to repentance, forgiveness, and the pursuit of holiness, to create the theological framework that undergirds much of Western Christianity today. He is the master theologian of painting with ashes. Not all of us turn our secret struggle with sin into one of the most popular works in history, but wounded healers find a way to make that journey of confession for themselves.

In the 12-step recovery fellowships, we have another cliché. It is the crystalized spiritual wisdom of millions of recovering people: "We are only as sick as our secrets."

The fourth step inventory asks us to write all of those secrets down on paper, and then in the fifth step, we confess them out loud to God, ourselves, and another human being. This becomes the list in steps eight and nine, where we go back and make amends "wherever possible" to all the people we have harmed.

It is often in this place of honest confession that so many falter along the spiritual path of healing. In Jesus' miracles, confession and forgiveness of sin are often connected with healing. James 5:16 tells us, "Confess your sins to one another and pray for one another, so that you may be healed" (NRSV), but rarely do Christians grapple with the power of this truth.

Is it possible to have our sins forgiven and yet not be healed? Are those one in the same phenomenon?

Catholics have long known the healing power of confession, one of their seven sacraments. But this is often lost among Protestant Christians. Protestants argue that we don't need a "middleman" to get to God. Through Jesus' death on the cross, which tore the temple veil in two, all humans now have equal access to God. Through Christ's wounded body, we can pass into the temple's Most Holy Place (or, Holy of Holies). We can confess our sin directly to God and receive forgiveness.

Yet if we take James 5 seriously, confession that leads to healing requires "one another." The sin that lies hidden in our hearts rots our souls from the inside out. That toxic guilt and shame trapped in our bodies can cause physical and mental illness. Yet when we can confess those things to God and another human, healing takes place.

One of the gifts of the Twelve Steps is the unwavering principle that recovery and healing from our woundedness are bound up with the honest confession of our sin to at least one other person. We don't need to tell everyone about our sin, like our friend Augustine, but we need to tell someone about it, someone we can trust. Also, this is not a onetime event. The idea of steps ten, eleven, and twelve, also called the maintenance steps, is that we keep doing daily what we did in the first nine steps. We continue to "take personal inventory and when we are wrong promptly admit it." This is why the importance of a "sponsor," or a guide who walks beside us in our journey of healing, is so essential to the recovery journey.

The importance of this part of our spiritual healing cannot be understated. Many lifelong church attendees never truly find healing because they miss this step. Without the experiencing of release provided through confession, we hold on to the darkest of human emotions, including resentment, fear, pride, lust, racism, sexism, and judgment. The fruits of the Spirit cannot grow in a heart still crowded with these roots of bitterness. Being able to truly experience love, joy, peace, patience, kindness, goodness, gentleness, and self-control requires a heart soil that has been cleansed from the weeds of secret sin.

In a sense, we need a soul janitor who can help us cleanse the toxic debris from our hearts. Secrets in the soul keep us sick. They are like poison that slowly kills us over time. Most Christians that crash and burn don't have that kind of safe relationship. We accumulate "little" sins in our souls. We convince ourselves they are no big deal, or even worse, that we are above the rules.

I've found in my own journey the importance of a soul friend. One of the many gifts of Celtic Christianity is the concept of the *anam cara*, or the "soul friend." *Anam* is the Gaelic word for soul, and *cara* is the word for friend. In the early Celtic church, there was a consistent theme of soul-love. A person who acted as a teacher, companion, sponsor, or spiritual guide was called an *anam cara*.

The origin of a soul friend was grounded in the idea of confession. This was a confidant to whom you confessed and revealed the hidden intimacies of your life. The *anam cara* was a safe person with whom you could share your soul.

I describe this person as a "soul janitor," someone (or some group) with whom you meet regularly. You can tell this person everything. It is someone outside the regular group of people whom you serve or work with, an individual who provides a space where you can cleanse the secrets of your soul. John Wesley figured out the need for soul janitors with his societies, classes, and bands. Safe groups were groups where people could get real and talk about "How goes it with your soul?" The healthiest Christians I know meet weekly with a person or group who helps them clean up the mess in their souls.

The health of the soul is a journey, not a destination. We never arrive. As Christians, we take this journey through a series of mentoring fellowships. We call this "discipleship." Discipleship is a one-on-one relationship of mutual blessing and an exchange of soul secrets. I often ask the people I coach if they have a soul janitor. I also ask them, "Who is discipling you?" And, "Whom are you discipling?" God's grace flows powerfully in and out of the stream of these relationships.

Maybe a simpler way to say this is that we all need a best friend. The kind of friendship I'm talking about is soul friendship—someone with whom you can just be you. Somebody whom you can tell what's going on in your heart and not be afraid of being judged. Someone to whom you can bare your deepest secrets. Those secrets often keep us trapped in guilt and shame. This is a person who will be with you through thick and thin, no matter what. This friendship should be an exchange of mutual blessing.

In my own journey toward healing, the most destructive sins of my life were not the ones I'd committed in my deep past, but the ones I have committed clean, sober, and active in ministry. As with Augustine, lust and sexual sin are an aspect of my core woundedness. The wiring for sex addiction didn't go away just because I stopped using drugs and alcohol. Sexual sin started to creep into my relationship in my new marriage to Jill. The difference was that there was no substance to medicate my agony, no magic bullet to take away my feelings of guilt, shame, and remorse.

By far the greatest addiction in the postmodern world is sex addiction. It's the secret struggle that millions of people we know are struggling with. One out of three men self-report that they are addicted to pornography. The pornography industry generates $12 billion of revenue each year. Sixty-six percent of internet-using eighteen- to thirty-four-year-old men look at online pornography at least once a month, and 70 percent of internet pornographic traffic occurs during the 9:00 a.m. to 5:00 p.m. workday. More than half of the men who identify themselves as evangelical Christians admit that they have an addiction to pornography and have used it within the last week for self-satisfaction. Worse, 55 percent of Christian pastors admitted to visiting a pornographic site. While it affects men on a larger scale, an increase in sex addiction among women has been growing steadily for years.[1]

In sexual recovery we have an acronym for our sobriety: MAP (masturbation, adultery, pornography). These are the physical ways we can act out, but the underlying problem is deeper and darker. It is the phenomenon of lust, and that force can express in many ways, even through workaholism, achievement, and doing ministry. Lust doesn't need you to take a substance; it can produce a high right in your own body, like a syringe or crack pipe attached to your flesh.

Lust is the thorn in my side for which I continue to need God's grace. It is in the daily yielding of that wound that never heals to Jesus that I find his power is made perfect in my weakness. (See 2 Corinthians 12:7–9.) And I can't carry the wound alone. I need an *anam cara*. I need a best friend.

At one point early in my ministry, my life was coming off the rails. I was a workaholic, using work like a drug so I didn't have to deal with myself. Churches love workaholic pastors. "Remember the Sabbath day, and keep it holy" is the only sin that pastors are expected to commit and get a standing ovation for (Exod 20:8 NRSV). Workaholism in no degree can ever help us become a wounded healer. It just makes us more wounded.

In my own woundedness, I had become a dry drunk, sexually. A "dry drunk" is someone who doesn't act on his or her lust but makes everyone else in his or her life miserable because of it. After a near-death experience, hospitalization, and the possibility of corrective surgeries on my digestive system, I found a "bottom that sufficiently horrified me," as one of our recovery clichés would say. I was leading a thriving church and was known in many circles as an effective minister. But I was completely dead inside.

I once heard my mentor Len Sweet say, "Everyone needs a best friend." He was referring to someone outside your spouse, work, and church community. Jesus seemed to have a best friend. It was Lazarus, the one whom, according to John 11:3, he "love[d]." Jesus went to Lazarus's house to kick back, to rest, maybe even to talk about how that dummy Peter tried to jump out of a boat and almost drowned himself last week.

Len's words made me realize that I didn't have a best friend like that. My best friends were all incarcerated, strung out, or dead. How does one go about finding a best friend? Do we stop random strangers on the street and strike up a conversation to see if they fit the bill?

After surviving the hospitalization and surgical ordeal, I did a radical thing: I prayed that God would give me a best friend. You may think, *Those kinds of prayer haven't always worked out for you, Beck.* God doesn't typically answer the way I expect. Angels in green suits with handcuffs are not outside the realm of possibility! I knew it was a gamble, but I went for it anyway.

Within a couple of days of that prayer, an older gentleman at the gym approached me. He just asked one of those awkward questions, "Hey, do you know so and so? Well, you look just like him." After a couple more encounters like that, we started to dig into some real conversations. My new friend was a financial advisor, but also a Christian, and we had lots of things in common. Before we knew it, we were having lunch together. In that first lunch, my new friend came clean. He had been struggling with sex addiction. I in turn told my story, and an instant bond was formed. Turns out he was praying for a best friend too!

Early in our relationship the Lord gave us the same word directly through prayer, "*I'm going to heal you through this relationship.*" So, my new BFF and I got together and got down to business. We committed to pray for each other daily. We also started sharing daily voice check-ins over the phone from our Bible readings. We decided that we would meet together weekly, often on his back porch, to share with each other the "how goes it with your soul" of our daily lives. Next, we planned out a weekend retreat. During that time, we took turns confessing every sordid sin of our lives from birth until the present. Then we prayed over each other to break soul ties and bind any demonic forces we felt were trying to establish a stronghold. We have sustained this level of commitment to each other for seven years now.

Our back-porch times are a holy space, a sanctuary, where we confess our sins one to another so that we might be healed, as directed in James 5:16. Two wounded healers, taking off our bandages, treating each other's wounds, giving ourselves fully to the wounded Healer, who sits silently between us at every meeting.

During the pandemic of 2020–21, we shifted to a weekly Face-Time. It takes effort and intentionality to grow and protect the connection, but the time we spend is the most healing thing in our lives. Even our virtual back-porch time has become a sanctuary of heart cleansing. The emotional, spiritual, and physical healing benefits are tremendous.

David and Jonathan were *anam cara*, soul friends. They knew a love that was "more wonderful than that of women" (2 Sam 1:26), a depth and realness, a commitment to each other. Relationships like this can be powerful instruments of healing.

True healing takes place in a matrix of safe relationships.

We are only as sick as our secrets. Confession in the safety of a trusting relationship is a healing balm. This is part of the magic that I believe happens in Alcoholics Anonymous or Celebrate Recovery meetings, or through a sponsor. The biblical principle of confession takes place in groups like these at times when people are brutally honest with themselves and with one another. These are places where we can just be real, talk about struggles, and get them out of our heads. We all need to tell our version of Augustine's *Confessions* and use our stories in ways that will bring healing to others who carry the same wounds. This is one reason I hope and pray that all people will discover they are in recovery.

12

THE GREAT CLOUD OF WITHNESSES

Without counsel purposes are disappointed: but in the multi-tude of counsellors they are established.

Proverbs 15:22 KJV

Penelope lay in the hollow of a tree for eight days, scalped, gutted, and left for dead. Her fellow travelers had journeyed to this land, hoping to find religious freedom, but she had discovered only pain and suffering. As soon as they'd come ashore into a world that was new to them, the challenges had begun. Her husband was so ill he could not move on, so their fellow travelers had left him behind and headed for New Amsterdam. Penelope stayed with her husband, try-ing to nurse him back to health, but they were attacked by a band of natives.

She crawled away from her husband's dead body, found refuge in the tree hollow, and survived by drinking its reservoir of rainwater. Two natives discovered her there, and after a heated debate around what to do, the older of the two decided to spare her life and bring her back to their village. There he cared for her, nurtured her healing, and encouraged the tribe to adopt her.

Later, a rescue party from the New Amsterdam colony was sent to retrieve her. When her physical recovery was complete, she settled in the English village of Gravesend on Long Island. There she mar-ried a prominent English settler named Richard Stout. Her old native friend would visit her frequently, and she never forgot the kindness and care that saved her life.

Years passed, and her family, along with other settlers decided to establish a new village in what is now Middletown, New Jersey. What they didn't know is that a band of Native Americans was planning to attack their new village. Her old friend visited her to inform her of the coming invasion. Her husband initially didn't heed her warning but later decided to prepare the other villagers.

After averting this near disaster, they decided to purchase the land from the Native Americans. Together the settlers and the natives held a two-day ceremony to celebrate their new peace agreement. They avoided the bloodshed and war that so many other settlements had experienced. The Monmouth Patent of 1664 guaranteed them religious and political freedom, and they lived peaceably as a mixed community of natives and settlers.

The settlement grew and became Middletown, the first settlement in the area. Penelope, who had survived against all odds, became known as the First Lady of Middletown. In 1668, she and her husband gathered others in the kitchen of their home to organize a new church. This kitchen gathering became the first Baptist Church of New Jersey. Eventually, Richard Stout became a large land proprietor and was appointed overseer of Middletown in 1669. He also served as an Indian commissioner.

By 1675, the couple had accumulated so much land that they were able to deed eighteen hundred acres to their heirs. Richard Stout died in 1705.

Penelope would become known throughout history as Penelope Van Princis Stout, more widely known as simply Penelope Stout. She bore ten children and lived a long, full life of 110 years. At the time of her death, she is said to have had hundreds of descendants. She became the matriarch of thousands. The Stouts originated families that spread across the United States, of whom there are many notable explorers, settlers, scholars, entrepreneurs, actors, and even a president. Penelope's daughter Mary had a great-granddaughter, Hannah Salter, who married Mordecai Lincoln. Hannah and Mordecai Lincoln are the great-great-grandparents of Abraham Lincoln.

Penelope Stout is also my great-grandmother on my maternal side, going back twelve generations.

Some scholars have sought to discredit Penelope's story as a founding myth, a narrative that evolved from oral tradition to a written captivity narrative. Since the eighteenth century, it has been transformed and retold, studied by early historians of New Jersey and by genealogists reconstructing the archaeology of the Stout lineage.

In "The Penelope Stout Story: Evolution of a New Netherland Narrative," Dr. Virginie Adane analyzes the story in depth. She draws together material consisting of the literature produced about Penelope Stout over the eighteenth and nineteenth centuries, historical works by antiquarians and historians on New Jersey, works published by genealogists seeking the origins of the Stout family, and the Penelope Stout story told as a children's tale. Adane considers the story an excerpt of Anglo-American folklore, which became disconnected from "official" New Netherland history. The story integrates a memory of the Dutch period of the early settlers, anglicized and melded into a more global Anglo-American tradition.[1]

While there do exist variations in the details of the lineage, by the late 1700s, the Stout family had taken up the practice of documenting the family line back to Richard and Penelope Stout, a practice continued by our family to this day.

For the first forty years of my life, I believed I was the product of incest. My mother and aunt convinced me that my grandfather was my biological father. Sadly, they experienced horrible sexual abuse and freely shared these stories with me.

Due to the nature of my birth circumstances, for the last forty years I've been completely disconnected from my family of origin. I had given up hope on knowing anything more than the story I was told. I took great comfort in knowing that God has always been a good Father and has provided a massive mixed-up family of sinners and saints called the church. But in another way, I was spiritualizing a problem that had a simple solution. I was afraid to say I cared, afraid to voice the pain that followed me like a shadow throughout my life. I would never let others see that fear. I hid the pain within relentless cycles of creativity.

My wife, Jill, often sees through my tough exterior. She has always sensed that deep down inside, questions about my origins bother me. Many times in our marriage, Jill has lent me her strength when I couldn't muster my own. In 2020 she gave me the gift of a DNA test for my fortieth birthday. My results came back matching me to thousands of genetic relationships. She did her research, reached out to my relatives, and connected me to a massive family tree I never knew I had.

My family tree has many branches, and the matriarchs and patriarchs of my line have carefully documented and preserved our lineage. They hold mammoth annual family reunions, belong to groups such as Daughters of the American Revolution and the Mayflower Society, and have an odd fascination with producing three-hundred-page books documenting family branches of our ancestry! Here's a little "CliffsNotes" version:

The Beck line goes back to John Beck (1770s, the farthest we can go without the proper documentation) and Rebecca Collins, daughter of Thomas Collins, who served under George Washington, wintered at Valley Forge, and fought at the battles of Trenton and Brandywine. Their son Jonathon married Mary Anne Orr, daughter of Thomas Orr and Mary Gatchell. The Gatchells were infamous troublemakers who came to Massachusetts in the 1600s. Thus, I have ancestral basis for my holy troublemaking. Jonathan, my eighth great-grandfather, ended up in Philadelphia, married to the daughter of William Penn's rope maker.

Edwin Augustus Beck, Jonathan's son, married Matilda Sanderson McCrum. He was an entrepreneur who started a lucrative company designing and building horse-drawn hearses and transporting the bodies of deceased persons to their final rest. Here is the connection to my entrepreneurial sensibility.

E. Augustus and Matilda helped found and were upstanding members of the Methodist Episcopal Church in Renovo, Pennsylvania, from 1832 to 1913. Being Wesleyan is baked into my blood and bones.

Going up the other direction of the tree, Matilda's great-grandmother was Hephzibah Stout, married to William McCrum.

Hephzibah was the daughter of Benjamin Stout, who was the son of Benjamin Stout and Hannah Bonham. Hannah is a granddaughter of Samuel Fuller, son of Edward, both of whom were on the *Mayflower*. Benjamin Stout is the grandson of Richard and Penelope Stout, my legendary very great-grandmother. Matilda McCrum's great-grandfather was John McClellan, who was one of the first commissioned officers in the Continental Army from Cumberland County, Pennsylvania. He died in November 1775 in Benedict Arnold's expedition to Canada. The McCrums, McClellans, and Buchanans (the family of John McClellan's mother) all came to America as the Jacobite rebellion went south, some by way of Northern Ireland.

My great-grandfather Russell I. Beck (1898–?), son of Edwin Beck and Nettie Gray, was the grandson of Edwin Augustus Beck. He was part of a group of Becks who moved from Pennsylvania into the Manhattan and Brooklyn boroughs of New York City. His sister Florence Beck was a professional ballroom dancer and instructor in Manhattan.

Russell I. Beck was the black sheep of the family. He ran away at fifteen (which made the newspaper, for some reason), got drafted into World War I, and came back married to my great-grandmother Edith. Edith was the daughter of a Moravian missionary to the West Indies, Rev. Jacob Howard. She's the one who lived in the bungalow in our backyard. Russell I. was an alcoholic, fathered children out of wedlock, and got mixed up in the Mafia (there are several newspaper clippings about his criminal activities and trials). He disappeared in his forties, his body never to be found.

Thus, my grandpa Russell H. Beck grew up with no father, married my gram Marion McDonald, went to fight in World War II, and came back and founded a home and lawn décor business in New York City until the move to Florida.

Jill's gift to me is this: my mother's claim that my grandfather was my biological father was proved false by my DNA test. One of the DNA matches led me to another family who traces back to early Irish-Scot settlers in the colony of Georgia. Last year, I met my biological father for the first time. While he was unwilling to take a

DNA test with me at that time and was not open to a relationship, his daughter, my half sister, was. We took a DNA test together to prove with 99.9 percent accuracy that we are siblings. At age forty, I learned for the first time the name of my biological father.

In my family line there are pioneers, revolutionaries, missionaries, entrepreneurs, sexual deviants, and alcoholics. Fullers, Stouts, McCrums, McClellans, Buchanans, Grays, and Becks helped form relationships with indigenous peoples and build the United States. They fought in the Revolutionary, Civil, and both world wars. They struggled and overcame incredible odds, survived hostile conditions, built businesses, and instigated criminal enterprises. All those dualities live in my blood still today.

All of this new information does not necessarily affect who I am in Christ or what I'm called to do in this world. Yet it does provide a backdrop for understanding the various polarities in my own being.

For orphaned, adopted, abused, and abandoned adult children, we can go through life feeling like "black sheep."

Yet even "black sheep" are sacred, beautiful, worthy, and valuable.

We are all part of a larger story. Maybe we feel we are cursed or even broken from our family tree; nevertheless, we are connected to and not isolated from this blended mess of humanity in profound ways.

The inner struggles we feel have been carried in our blood for generations. Something beyond us, but in us, pushes us both to perform incredible feats of love and to inflict harm, to pioneer new territories and to burn down the villages of others.

I spent my youth trying to survive with no parental support or family network. These negative instincts are not easily unlearned. I was deeply deformed in faulty mental attitudes. Now, as I'm corresponding and Zooming with relatives I never knew I had, I'm feeling a new sense of peace. I feel connected to humanity, not just in a spiritual way, which is real and powerful, but in a flesh-and-blood, genetic way. I also feel a deep sense of connection with this country, both its positive and negative dimensions.

Even a bastard born addicted in the NICU of a Gainesville, Florida, hospital can carry the story of a whole nation in his bones. There is a deep interrelatedness in us all. *Ubuntu.* In a pandemic era, when our nation was shown to worship at the throne of a god whose guiding principles seemed to be the "affordable loss" of disposable human life, or "survival of the fittest," wounded healers who paint with ashes can point us back to a God who is self-defined by love and care for the vulnerable (Ps 68:5). Those who died daily from COVID-19 are our kin, our own flesh and blood, our brothers and our sisters.

All of this depends on each of us having the courage to ask our own tough questions, the ones that we pretend don't bother us. It requires us to stop spiritualizing our pain and instead do the relational work that brings actual healing. Each of us must answer Jesus' question, "Do you want to get well?"

Even the cursed branches of a family tree can bear fruit in the power of a God of unfailing love.

What has carried me these forty years of life as a branch broken from a family tree is the great cloud of "withnesses" who adopted me into their family. In *11 Indispensable Relationships You Can't Be Without*, my mentor, theologian Leonard Sweet, shows that the real meaning of life is not about journeys or arrivals. It is about relationships. Sweet writes, "Life is a handicap event. We can't get to our destination without the help of others." He calls these eleven indispensable relationships "withnesses." It's a play on the word *marturos* ("martyr" or "witness"). Jesus chose a group of disciples to "be with him" (Mk 3:14).

Withness must come before witness.[2] We all need a great cloud of withnesses (see Heb 12:1). Sweet shows that every person needs a community of people who will walk with us in our journey. He includes some examples:

1. Nathan (editor): Someone who can stick the finger in your face, call you out, and tell you when you're not speaking with a Jesus voice.

2. Jonathan (true friend): A loyal friend who loves you as they love themselves, the one who never leaves your side, the *anam cara*, a "soul friend" and "second self."

3. Jethro (butt-kicker): Someone who kicks you in the pants, motivates you to fulfill God's mission, and blesses you forward into the future.

4. Timothy (protégé): An heir and an apprentice, usually a younger and less mature version of yourself.

5. Barnabas (encourager): A person who is in your corner, encouraging you to press on, believing in you even when you don't believe in yourself, pouring their heart into you.

6. Peter or Paul (Yoda): A mentor, a guru, a coach, spiritual teacher/director who is usually older and more mature who guides us to complete the mission to which God has called us.

7. Deborah (back-coverer): A protector and defender, who when people sneak attack with criticisms and back-stabbing, they've got your back.

8. Zacchaeus (reject): An oddball, street-urchin, cast-off, social misfit, someone who needs something from you rather than gives anything to you.

9. Rhoda (little one): A child, with big faith, a young one, who keeps you small and in touch with the wonderful world of "make-believe."

10. VIPs (Lydia and Lazarus, rich and poor): A Lydia is a sponsor, a patron, a provider and a partner, someone who gives of their own means to further the mission. A Lazarus is the skin-diseased, disabled, beggar, who lives off the scraps of others, the one whose condition breaks our hearts and motivates us to press on.

11. Jerusalem (place): Every person needs to go local, to become a native, to live a landscape that we call home, a zip code that we love so much we weep over it.

12. The invisible 12th (paraclete): All humans will ultimately fail us at some point, but Christians have a final invisible withness . . . the Holy Spirit. We need the "Comforter" to bear our burdens, carry our loads, and give us life, to be our armor of light, spiritual bodyguard, and battle companion.

Ubuntu. We are persons through other persons. Or in the words of Fred Rogers, this great cloud of withnesses make up the ones who "love us into being."

<hr>

If life is a handicap event, we need a community to help us along as we become wounded healers. This truth became very real to me at one point in a state-run rehab. I was blindfolded, following a rope through a maze. It was an exercise that the director of the rehabilitation center had put together. You had to keep your hand on the rope the entire time. Weaving through trees and obstacles, stepping over the bodies of colleagues on the ground. A group of volunteers was on standby in case we needed help. Every once in a while, one of them would say, "Make sure to step over the dead bodies of those who fell before you."

The goal was to find the end of the maze and escape alive. The problem was the maze had no end. I made my circuit around the maze; my typical Enneagram type 8, driven, challenger self, had to be the first of course. But I could tell the game was rigged. This was a trick of some kind. This maze had no end.

So, I stopped and stuck up my hand. Quickly, one of the volunteers put her hand on my shoulder, "Yes?" she asked.

"This is a trick. This maze has no end," I huffed.

"Okay. What are you asking?" the voice replied.

"I need help," I responded.

"Come with me," the volunteer said, as she took my hand off the rope and led me out of the maze. I discovered that was actually the whole point of the exercise. There was no way out of the maze. The only way to get free was to stop and ask for help.

That was a powerful lesson in itself, but what happened next is burned into my memory forever. As someone who had been freed from the maze, I now had the vantage point of watching my colleagues navigate its challenges. My fellow rehab residents, blindfolded, traveled around the circuit of the maze again and again. An hour passed. Then two hours. Three. Not a single person had yet considered the only way out was to stop and ask for help. Some got pissed and stormed off. Others stopped and shouted obscenities in frustration. Some lay on the ground and became the dead bodies.

It is hard for people to ask for help. It is a deeply intimate experience that requires vulnerability. One of the ways the ashes of my childhood was a gift was awareness that I was going through life with no tools. I knew I lacked the parental and familial relationships that the majority of people had. Because of this, it has been easy for me to embrace the gift of mentorship.

I am who I am today because of the great cloud of withnesses who "loved me into being." One of the few things I have done right in my recovery journey has been to ask for help. In the 12-step fellowships we say to "find someone who has what you want, and then do what they do." That is how we determine who we will ask to be our sponsor. A sponsor is a mentor who walks alongside us as we journey through the steps. My sponsor taught me the "design for living."

After turning my life over to new management, making my inventory, confessing all my deep dark secrets, and asking for God to take away my character defects, now I had to make a list of all the people I had harmed and then make amends to each one. This could be disastrous without the guidance of a sponsor. My sponsor counseled me in how to deal with each of these difficult situations. Not only did this mean people we'd harmed emotionally, physically, or sexually, but those we had harmed financially. We pulled my credit report and went through each item . . . lots of them! I called companies, who offered settlement amounts in exchange for removal from my report. Over the course of years, I paid every single debt and began a debt-free policy with my finances.

That is the gift of sponsorship. I have discovered that it works in every dimension of life. If I was going to be a good pastor, I needed to learn from someone "who had what I wanted." So, I took a gamble and asked the Reverend Walter Edwards to meet me for lunch. Walter was a retired district superintendent who had pastored churches for fifty years. If someone knew about how to do this gig right, it was Walter. During our first lunch I popped the question, like that lost rehab resident in a maze: "Can you help me?" I asked Walter to be my mentor, and he said yes.[3]

We began meeting together weekly for lunch. I assaulted him with questions, and he patiently listened and then asked questions in response to my questions. He suggested books that I should read, and we talked about those. He helped me understand the deep contradictions in the Bible but showed me how it was still true. He showed me who John Wesley was, and why his theological pathway was the right one for me. He prayed for me and gave me his wisdom week after week for over a decade, and all it cost was the price of buying him lunch. Walter became my Master Yoda. He was the sponsor of my pastoral life up until the day he died. Walter passed peacefully into the arms of Jesus at 87 years old just weeks from this writing.

I applied this wisdom to my educational journey as well. When a professor seemed to really know his or her stuff, and live it, I asked if I could take him or her to lunch. I learned much more outside of classrooms than in them. Breaking bread around meal tables, sitting in a park, or hanging in the parking lot after class is how the deeper relational wisdom came out. I did this as an undergraduate all the way through my doctoral work. Some of those mentors remain close friends and guides to this day.

As my ministry expanded, my relationship with Jorge Acevedo continued to grow. His heart for those "no one else wants or sees" is also my heart. So, I took his hand as a mentor and guide and agreed to serve as a kind of mini-bishop over an area network of churches. As someone who has lived the role of "heroic solo leader" for part of his ministry, Jorge continues to help me rein myself in, take care of myself, and do ministry in teams.

In Portland during one of my doctoral studies gatherings, our group of students was walking through the city from the classroom to a place to have dinner. Our mentor, Len Sweet, was walking all by himself, which I thought was odd. I thought that perhaps no one had the courage to approach him in an informal way. This was my opportunity. I caught up to him, matched his stride, and said, "Hey, Dr. Sweet, can I ask you something?"

"Sure, Michael. Go ahead," he said in his distinct, booming voice.

"I'm wondering if you would be willing to be my mentor," I blurted out, awkward as a virgin in the backseat of a car on prom night.

"Michael, I'm always so surprised how few students actually ask me that question." He smiled. "Of course I would be honored to be your mentor."[4]

From then on, our relationship grew outside the classroom in beautiful ways. Every person needs a Yoda and a rabbi. You sit under your rabbi's teaching and learn his or her voice and theological posture. Your rabbi is someone who challenges you. You must read every book he or she has written—not an easy task with Len, who has written more than sixty books, and counting. In some ways one aspect of my calling has been to take the deep thinking of Len Sweet and to translate some of his more complex ideas for ministry on the front lines. As a onetime president and a lifelong seminary educator, Len continues to help me develop in my own work as a professor.

Perhaps some of the most significant mentoring relationships in my life are reverse mentorships from my own team, most of whom are laypersons: Eric, Karen, Dwayne, Nicole, Brittany, Jack, Kim, Chelsy, Adam, Piper, Jennifer, and Kelly. These faithful followers are stepping into their own callings and making good on the ordinations that have occurred in the waters of their baptisms. In this perichoretic, shared approach to leadership, we are constantly playing our parts in the continuous dance of follower and leader, teacher and student, sheep and shepherd. Many times, I am in the role of listener and learner rather than teacher.

I intentionally seek out young leaders who are doing crazy, amazing stuff, and I ask them to mentor me. These are my Rhodas (See Acts 12:13–15). While some of them find this relationship awkward at first, over time these have become very fruitful relationships for both of us. Trying to understand what emerging generations are doing, how they do it, and why puts me in a continual space of learning. These younger leaders help close the blind spots in my own approach to life and ministry. Secretly, I'm learning more from my doctoral students than I am teaching them. Staying up to speed with their work keeps me on the edge of what's happening in an ever-growing knowledge base.

We all need a great cloud of witnesses, and these are some of mine.

PART FOUR:
FLOURISHING

13

IMAGINATION—FINDING YOUR SUPERPOWER

*Now to him who by the power at work within us is able to ac-
complish abundantly far more than all we can ask or imagine,
to him be glory in the church and in Christ Jesus to all generations, forever and ever. Amen.*

Ephesians 3:20–21 NRSV

Most people falsely assume that Elon Musk is a rigid logician, whose engineer mind functions robotically, like a computer processing code. A deeper look at his life and achievements show that his true superpower lies in the power of his wild imagination and the guts to take risks. Musk can imagine bigger than most, but then he finds ways to make those imaginings a reality.

Musk was born on June 28, 1971, in Pretoria, Transvaal, South Africa. His mother was a Canadian model and dietitian. His father was a South African electromechanical engineer, pilot, sailor, consultant, and property developer. The oldest of three children, Elon grew up in a fairly stable household until his parents divorced when he was nine. Musk chose to live with his father in Pretoria but later regretted that decision, reporting that his father had become "a terrible human being."[1]

Musk describes a kind of boredom with life, and particularly with the educational system. He spent more time imagining what could be than studying the well-worn paths of what is. Because he felt like an awkward child who tended toward introversion, he was bullied throughout his childhood and once hospitalized after a group of boys threw him down a flight of stairs. All of this led him to an existential crisis as an adolescent.

When Musk turned ten, a Commodore VIC-20 thrust him into the world of computing. A self-taught computer programmer by the age of twelve after studying programming manuals, he developed and then sold the code of a BASIC-based video game he had created, called *Blastar*, for approximately $500. That would not be his last entrepreneurial enterprise.

Today, Musk is a centibillionaire and one of the richest people in the world. Not only is he a business magnate, industrial designer, and engineer; he was the mind behind PayPal; founder, CEO, CTO, and chief designer of SpaceX; early investor, CEO, and product architect of Tesla, Inc.; founder of the Boring Company; cofounder of Neuralink; and cofounder and initial cochairman of OpenAI. Most recently he has set his imagination on establishing the first colony on Mars by 2050.

The angst and struggle of his youth led Musk to dedicate himself to ventures that could change the world. He spent his college days using imagination to think outside the current systems. He dreamed up what could be and designed different pathways to get there. The bullied little boy, child of divorce, considered by teachers to be less intelligent than his grade school peers, is changing this world and has dreams for another, seeking to make humans a multi-planetary species in a space-faring civilization. Musk paints with ashes, and his imagination is his superpower. It has given us fast-accelerating electric cars and reusable rockets and has catalyzed a new era of space-traveling possibilities.

Perhaps, imagination is the true superpower of dreamers like Martin Luther King Jr. As a young pastor, King rehearsed and memorized his spellbinding sermons for fifteen to twenty hours every week. He wasn't much of a traditional "shepherd" type, but his preaching was so exceptional that the churches he served always grew. For him, faithful preaching was an act of shepherding love, and his people loved him for it. Preaching is an imaginative art form.

When Rosa Parks was arrested for refusing the bus driver's order, King was propelled into speaking to a large crowd, including television networks, at Holt Street Church. He was being asked to speak at one of the largest venues of his life, including national media, with little preparation. He anguished about what to say, but ultimately during his speech, he moved into "improvisation." He let go of himself and delivered one of the most powerful oratory presentations of his life. King honed this skill in his many speeches, sermons, and letters.

This prepared King to deliver the speech originally titled "Normalcy, Never Again" which we know today as the "I Have a Dream" speech. It is one of the great oral proclamations of history, perhaps second only to Jesus' Sermon on the Mount. King preached before 250,000 people gathered at the feet of Abraham Lincoln's memorial, and millions more gathered around their television sets nationwide. He and his aides carefully crafted the manuscript he would deliver. What many people don't know is that Martin wasn't really inspired by the manuscript himself. At one point during the speech, before the largest crowd of his life, in the most important proclamation he would ever utter, he decided to go off script and improvise.

During the "I Have a Dream" speech, as you watch the sermon, you can see the moment King goes off manuscript, when he says, "Go back to Mississippi . . ." In the moment, as he grasped for words, the great gospel singer Mahalia Jackson yelled, "Tell 'em about the dream, Martin!" The moment is so powerful you can feel the presence of the Holy Spirit through the old black-and-white footage as King begins, "I have a dream . . ."

The most powerful piece of the message, and the greatest oratory masterpiece of all time, was completely improvised, springing from the imagination of the prophet in real time.

By using imagination to envision a new future, and metaphors that allowed others to experience it, King led an entire nation down a new creation path. Amid fragmentation and failures and the uncertainty of what might come, he stood boldly pointing us to a vision of the new creation come to earth.

Whoever said, "The true sign of intelligence is not knowledge but imagination" was onto something. One fascinating strand that runs through the lives of each of the individuals I've explored so far is that each one in some way was or is able to use his or her imagination in a transformative way.

To one extent or another, imagination is a superpower we all have.

Imagination urges all wounded healers to paint with ashes. Sometimes it lies dormant or gets educated out of us. Perhaps the excelled use of imagination is somehow connected to childhood traumas. When the world as we know it is hard and painful, we dream of a world that could be different. When parental figures are less than ideal and nurturing, we envision relationships that could be possible. Abandoned, orphaned, abused, or neglected children seem to get a head start in honing the superpower of imagination. Because the world is traumatic and harmful, we use imagination to escape and rework our experience. Children in trauma situations can use imagination as a kind of coping mechanism.

We learn to dream up and play forth new worlds. We create imaginary friends and scenarios. We throw ourselves into entrepreneurial ventures, using imagination to dream up new products and services, then find ways to make them real in the world.

We hone this superpower to survive oppressive situations as children, but as adults we learn to use it to transform lives, communities, and the world. Imagination can be a force both for good or for evil. It is a double-edged sword.

Becoming like a little child to enter the kingdom is one of the most fascinating messages of Jesus' teaching (see Matt 18:1–3). While entire books are written on this idea alone, we can obviously see that humility, dependence, innocence, and trust are components of what children possess often lacking in adults. But I believe it is imagination that Jesus intends the most. The religious leaders that Jesus found himself in conflict with, as well as the disciples who followed him, were stuck in rigid mental models about God, humanity, and how the world worked. In the words of ordained rabbi, family therapist, and systems theorist Edwin Friedman, they were experiencing "imaginative gridlock."[2]

Jesus consistently challenged these hardened mindsets in his actions and teachings, inviting his listeners to expand their minds, pay attention to the wonder all around them, and use imagination to see possibilities that were hidden just below the surface.

In the previous chapter I wrote about the great cloud of "witnesses." What does the writer of Hebrews say about the "great cloud of witnesses"?

> Therefore, since we are surrounded by so great a cloud of witnesses, let us also lay aside every weight and the sin that clings so closely, and let us run with perseverance the race that is set before us, looking to Jesus the pioneer and perfecter of our faith, who for the sake of the joy that was set before him endured the cross, disregarding its shame, and has taken his seat at the right hand of the throne of God. (12:1–2 NRSV)

Not only do we need this community of support—we are "persons through other persons"—but we need to focus on Jesus, the One who is called the *archegos*, the "pioneer, author, or first-one" of our faith. The Greek word here is the closest we get in the biblical witness to the concept of an innovator. Jesus pioneered a new way to be with God. Jesus blazed the trail of new creation. Jesus altered the state of the cosmos through his life, death, and resurrection. Now, because he has sent us his Spirit, we too can function as *archegos*, pioneers, innovators, always following in the slipstream of Jesus, and as we do so, blazing trails of healing love within God's new creation.

The mind of God imagined forth the cosmos. We existed in the imagination of God before God spoke light and put on flesh, to be with us and heal us. Part of our healing is God's redemption and renewal of our imaginations. In Christ we can actually return to that of a little child. We can take on childlike characteristics and imagine and play forth new possibilities.

I wonder if the little boy growing up in Nazareth, the one whose parents had a sketchy backstory, ever experienced trauma or pain. Did the people in his hometown gossip about his mother and her story of angelic visits and miraculous conception? Was Jesus ever picked on by the town bullies? Did his father's work as a *tekton* (artisan or craftsman), draw the scoffing of the royal or priestly well-to-dos? While we can't know this for sure through the biblical witness, our woundedness binds us in our universal experience as human beings and helps us imagine the kinds of trauma that may have shaped the little boy from Nazareth. If Jesus didn't experience the pain of loss and trauma that all humans face to some degree, could we really say he lived a fully human life?

I believe that in Jesus' full humanness, he did experience wounding in his early years, as all human beings do. Perhaps it shaped his own imagination.

It's a running joke among clergy that Jesus would get thrown out of the church today for his radical ideas and wild imagination. He would never make it through many modern ordination processes. In a sad way, we have exiled the pioneer gift set, described by Jonny Baker, director of mission education for the Church Mission Society, as "the gift of not fitting in."[3]

Because entrepreneurial types employ different thinking processes and use imagination, improvisation, and intuition rather than causal logic, they are often silenced or marginalized in the church. Fixed denominational systems that like the well-oiled institutional machinery to run smoothly often dislike troublesome questions that disrupt the status quo. We cherish the stabilizers of systems, not the disrupters. We need good company women and men who will mind the store, not revolutionaries running around in their imaginations all day. Yet there was nothing about the ministry of Jesus that was stabilizing or nonthreatening to the religious system.

Unfortunately, these tendencies close the gates on many wounded healers. They stand outside. They don't know the secret gate code. Perhaps this contributes to the church's identity as a place of harm rather than healing. Systems that reward the good stewards of the status quo create power hierarchies. Those who mind the store will begin to climb the corporate ladder to success. Power is a corrupting force, and very few are able to give it away once they attain it. Great evil is perpetuated in maintaining hierarchies. Church history is rife with examples. Yet our *archegos* is known for downward mobility, self-emptying, and vulnerability.

It is impossible to paint with ashes without imagination.

We can only stand before the blank canvas with a brush in our hands. It takes imagination to unleash creativity. Perhaps this is one of the saddest blemishes of the modern church: it is a place of anti-creativity. It's a place where troublesome "what could be" questions are silenced, where the contributions of many people are diminished.

If any community in the world should be a place of flourishing imagination and creativity, it is the church. We follow a God who imagined creation and brought it forth by an ultimate act of creative word and will. We believe in an enfleshed God, who in the fullness of time, came to us as a humble carpenter's son, born in a feeding trough for animals, a wound-bearing God who was crucified, rose again, and now sits on the throne of the cosmos. We can't even access thinking about God without imagination: his ways are higher than our ways, and his thoughts above our thoughts (Isa 55:9).

I believe recovering imagination, innovation, and entrepreneurship in the church is the key to a thriving future. As my friend Len Wilson has written in *Greater Things*, it is Christian innovation in the power of the Holy Spirit, that allows us to be part of the cosmic ingredients for a new creation. Jesus didn't say you will do "normal things" or "status quo things," but "greater things."[4]

This is not more conflation of Christian teaching with the myth of progress. Rather, new creation is achieved through the path of death and resurrection. Hebrews 12 also tells us about the cross that comes when we pioneer new paths. If we follow in the slipstream of Jesus, there is no alternate ending. Carrying the cross will always be our reality.

Imagination as resurrection is not about replication of what was before, but continuity. It's a metamorphosis. The same content is now newly imbued with resurrection life. The body of Jesus is actually raised from an empty tomb, but in unfathomably different form.

A church of wounded healers will need to be the same, but different.

Against all odds, I have resisted the domestication of my imagination. When I was called a bastard, I dreamed of a day when I would be called beloved. When I was mocked for being the child of a street-walking prostitute, I believed that the world should and could be different. When judges, court systems, and police officers told me I would be resigned to a fate of lifelong incarceration or death, I imagined alternative ways that this could be untrue. And when I covenanted to give my life to a denomination that has in some ways hidden me and in which I refuse to climb corporate ladders, I dreamed up congregations who believed in "being church differently." We imagined them, then brought them into being.

I'm currently involved in revitalizing multiple congregations, writing books, creating a new house of studies at a seminary, training and consulting, teaching courses, and cultivating new Christian communities across the land, all because I am a follower of Jesus. I live in the slipstream of the great *archegos*. Everywhere he goes there are trails of new creation blazed in his wake. I live in the wake of Jesus' creativity.

I'll let you in on the secret of so many who have learned to paint with ashes: the real superpower is Spirit-inspired imagination.

———≈≈≈≈———

Jeanne-Marie Bouvier de la Motte-Guyon (1648–1717) practiced a devotional posture that some have called the "inward way." Guyon published a book called *A Short and Very Easy Method of Prayer* in 1685. She anchored the central premise of the book on Jesus' teaching that the "kingdom of heaven is within you" (Luke 17:21 KJV). Guyon proposed that the Lord's presence is not found outwardly but through an inward journey of *attentive silence*.

The publication incited the king of France to accuse her of immorality and label her a heretic. She was imprisoned by local authorities and moved around from prison to prison. She was frequently assaulted and kept in decrepit rooms under deplorable conditions. Ultimately, she was moved to solitary confinement in the notorious Parisian Bastille. For seven years she was falsely incarcerated and abused. When she was finally exonerated and declared innocent of her charges, she was so physically degraded that she had to be carried out of the prison on a litter.

The sustaining force throughout her imprisonment was humble, silent prayer. The inward way of *attentive silence* is a means of communicating with God in humility, inward simplicity, and contemplation. During her physical confinement, it was this focused, intentional prayer-as-communion, that protected her sanity and helped her sustain hope.

Guyon wrote that the silence of the soul "becomes both a wonderful transmission and receiving of divine communication." She believed that silence before God was a path to true humility and is the same posture that Jesus encouraged in his disciples, who were to become "like little children" (Matt 18:3). The practice requires one to push past all the distractions of the senses to enter a state of quiet solitude. Through this practice a transformation of the soul can take place, an active response to outward trauma, conflict, confusion, or unrest.[5]

The practice is most closely aligned with a particular form of contemplation. The distinction is that rather than meditating on a text or eliminating every thought, one actively seeks the presence of Christ within. Unlike supplication, meditation, or praise, this is a surrender of the prayer of the heart to the will of God. We are turning our full attention to the activities taking place in our innermost being. There we find the Spirit. For Guyon, contemplation was an active seeking of the presence of Christ within.[6]

The Spaniard and onetime soldier who converted to Christ, Saint Ignatius of Loyola (1491–1556), is known as the founder of the Jesuit Order. After practicing a severe form of asceticism for a time, he turned to inner quiet and reflection. One aspect of Ignatian spirituality was a "turn to the world." The movement inward should flow out to engage the world outward. Jesuits were a missional movement. They were traveling preachers who set up free schools, catechized, and baptized new believers outside the reach of the inherited church.

Ignatius also pioneered a distinct form of contemplation. He believed that God could speak to us directly through our imaginations as well as thoughts and memories. In the Ignatian way, praying with the imagination is called contemplation. This form of contemplation is an active way of praying that engages the mind and heart and stirs up thoughts and emotions. Other spiritual traditions understand contemplation as a way of praying that frees the mind of all thoughts and images. Through Ignatian contemplation, the Holy Spirit makes Jesus present to us in a direct, personal, and evocative way.[7]

Here's how the practice of Guyon and Ignatius converge in me. The evolution of my prayer life has brought me back to my Garden of Eden: my grandparents' backyard. For me, the inner move of attentive silence happens in hour-long sessions in the morning prayer chamber. I minimize as much outer sensory stimuli as possible. I close my eyes and center on adoring Jesus. I tune out the mental chatter until all the thoughts about to-do lists, challenges, and appointments are silent in my soul. Sometimes I have to focus on a gospel story or a word until the chatter is silenced.

What happens next is what I can only describe as a kind of visionary trance or dreamlike state. This is what I believe Paul referred to as being "in the Spirit" (see, for example, 1 Cor 14:2 NRSV). I describe it in recovery language as "conscious contact with my higher power," as I pray "only for the knowledge of his will for me and the power to carry that out." It is a means of direct communication with Jesus.

Then, I see visions, images, or scenes. Many times, I start in my grandparents' backyard, climbing the old Japanese plum tree, sitting on the stone wall where I preached my first sermons to invisible crowds, or somehow, I find a miniature version of myself swimming in the birdbath, looking up from under the water as hundreds of bumblebees drop down and skim across the surface. After a time of this, Jesus leads me into different scenes. Some of them have to do with people in my life. Sometimes they're related to ministry. Sometimes I get a direct download, like a book chapter or sermon idea. This time can take many forms. But I can only call these forms of revelation. When I receive them, I act upon them. This is a way that Jesus is managing my life, accessing my mind through imagination. Jesus directs my daily activities through these times of contemplation.

I first discovered the ability to do this in my solitary confinement cell. At times the anxiety was so great that I felt like I was coming to the edge of madness. As inmates kicked the doors, a chorus of howls and screams would erupt. Some threw feces from the chow slots to provoke the guards to beat them into submission. I would stop, breathe, and meditate. Suddenly I was no longer in the cell but freed from my incarcerated body. It was as though I were traveling in the Spirit. In those moments, I felt connected to God.

If my brain were being scanned during these times of imaginative prayer, it would probably light up the different regions where the magic of imagination happens. Some might minimize this as mere imagination and not real. But for me it's a state of hyper-realness, not make-believe. Those times of communion sustain me through the daily struggles and challenges of life. Perhaps prayer and imagination are not as disconnected as one might think.

Neuroscientists have used fMRI (functional magnetic resonance imaging) to measure brain activity during different forms of cognition. The default mode network (DMN) is a system of connected brain regions, incorporating parts of the prefrontal, parietal, and temporal cortices that show joint activation (or deactivation) in connection with particular mental functions. The DMN is especially active, when one engages in introspective activities such as daydreaming, imagination, contemplating the past or the future, or thinking about the perspective of someone else. The DMN is active when a person is awake but in a resting state, not engaged in any demanding, externally oriented mental task—hence the word "default."[8]

Research shows that how we perceive the world around us is deeply affected by our imagination in a significant way. The thoughts that emerge in our imagination can alter our actual perception. The DMN also plays an important role in how we respond to beauty, selectively engaging with highly moving visual art. Contemplation weakens the brain's "Me Center," a region associated with gut feelings and fight or flight. DMN modulation can decrease negative emotions and feelings relating to the self, promoting more self-esteem and in turn happiness.[9]

While there are conflicting research and varying interpretations around brain activity and different forms of cognition, this could in some degree explain the science behind Guyon's practice of attentive silence or Ignatius' praying with the imagination. The healing properties amid trauma, and the reorganization of one's reality in a deeper spiritual sense are at some level verifiable.

Cognitive-behavioral therapists use a tool of imagination called "cognitive reframe" to help clients heal. We have a tendency to view situations, experiences, ideas, and emotions through a lens of victimhood. Cognitive reframing is the process in which these situations or thoughts are challenged and then changed, by imagining new perspectives and possibilities. Imagination has the power to reshape our reality.

Imaginative prayer is a primary way to paint with ashes. It's the gift Jesus gives us to survive our childhoods, and now Jesus uses it to bring healing to others. I consider this to be what he meant when he said the gift of prayer is none other than the presence of God . . . "the Holy Spirit to those who ask" (Luke 11:13).

I don't always do this well. There are periods where the traumas in my life drown out the stillness. There are dry times too, where I feel as if God has left me. I go through the motions of the activity, but the presence isn't there. When that happens, it means there is usually something in me that is blocking me from hearing God, not that God is absent.

God communicates to me primarily through my imagination, just as he did when I was a little boy. This is my journey toward "becom[ing] like little children" (Matt 18:3). But this practice is followed up by action, or Ignatius' "turn to the world." The "action" is less about *doing* and more about *being*. Imaginations become embodied realities not by our work but by the power of the Spirit. As we "abide" in the true vine, we begin to bear fruit (see John

15 NRSV). And faithfulness always precedes fruitfulness. This is about "presencing" Jesus in community with others. This resembles improvisation, but in practice, it's more about joining what God is doing than making something happen. A new entrepreneurial venture, creating a network, planting a church, facilitating a counseling session, delivering a sermon, writing a book, or simply trying to make a stranger smile, can all spring from times of imaginative prayer.

In seeking to be a channel of the Holy Spirit, doing comes into being.

People like King and Musk show us that imagination is not enough. We also need courage and the faith to believe that what we imagine can be a reality. Not faith in ourselves, but faith in the Christ within us. As Ignatius discovered, spiritual practices that connect us with Jesus somehow spill out into the world through our lives.

That said, wherever imagination soars, so do its critics. Not everyone appreciates innovative people who think and do differently. Honing our superpower may also cause us to be accused of shepherd malpractice.

14

SHEPHERD MALPRACTICE

*Now all the tax collectors and sinners were coming near to
listen to [Jesus]. And the Pharisees and the scribes were
grumbling and saying, "This fellow welcomes sinners and eats
with them." So, he told them this parable: "Which one of you,
having a hundred sheep and losing one of them, does not
leave the ninety-nine in the wilderness and go after the one
that is lost until he finds it? When he has found it, he lays it on
his shoulders and rejoices.*

Luke 15:1–5 NRSV

The coal miners in Borinage, Belgium, nicknamed the slightly odd
young man with a heart for the weary "Christ of the coal yards." It
was 1879, and after failing out of studies to be a priest, Vincent had
accepted a post as a missionary in the coal mining village of Petit
Wasmes in the center of Borinage. He thought it peculiar that any
representative of Christ would dress or live in affluence among the
deeply impoverished people. So, he offered his comfortable room at
a bakery to a homeless person and moved himself into a small hut.
His bed was straw. He ate what little bit he could to survive but
found ways to ensure others had sufficient food.

Vincent Willem van Gogh was born on March 30, 1853, in the
small village of Groot-Zundert, Holland. His father, Theodorus van
Gogh, was a Calvinist minister, and his mother, Anna Cornelia Car-
bentus van Gogh, had a flare for the artistic. A year before Vincent's
birth, the couple had lost a stillborn child. They gave Vincent the
same name as his deceased older sibling but were never quite able

to accept the death of their first son. This created a lack of intimacy between Vincent and his mother.

Vincent's sister-in-law, Johanna van Gogh-Bonger, reported that Vincent felt rejected. He had a moody, melancholy disposition, was seldom happy, and was combative and argumentative. In one of his letters to his brother Theo, later in life, Vincent wrote, "My youth was gloomy and cold and sterile under the influence of the rayon noir [black ray]."[1]

Vincent felt a calling to the ministry, and in May 1877, he moved to Amsterdam to study theology. His family was supportive and even hired a tutor to help him prepare for the theological examinations. Vincent had a passionate personal relationship with God. Yet, he felt preparation for the ministry was disconnected, dispassionate, and overly formal. Subsequently, he was not a good student and dropped out in July 1878. He decided to take a different route as an evangelical missionary, which offered a shorter program of study in Brussels.[2]

Van Gogh became deeply impressed with the fifteenth-century book by Thomas à Kempis, *The Imitation of Christ* (c. 1418–1427), written originally in Latin.[3] The stress of the devotional book was to live one's life in the manner of Christ, especially following Christ's example of humility, lowliness, discipline, prudence, inward consolation, and the embracing of misery. It was an early version of the concept of "accepting hardships as the pathway to peace," from the Serenity Prayer, cited in chapter 2. Vincent was so taken by the work that he suggested only it and the Bible should be read at all.

This certainly shaped how the "Christ of the coal yards" pursued a life of intense self-discipline, seeking to live among the miners, who were the honest, hardworking, suffering poor, the sort of people among whom Christ had walked. Unfortunately, this put him at odds with church doctrine. Determined to live the life of Christ, he purposely sought out the most run-down hut in the village, gave away his clothes and bed, and lived on scraps of food. He personally went down into the mines to experience the hard lives of the noble poor. Perhaps in his eyes, he was imitating how Christ had gone against the religious leaders of his own day. Nevertheless, the church did not take too kindly to his ministry among the poor.

The 1879–1880 report from the Synodal Board of Evangelization of the Union of Protestant Churches of Belgium gives the official view:

> The experiment of accepting the services of a young Dutchman, Mr. Vincent van Gogh, who felt himself called to be an evangelist in the Borinage, has not produced the anticipated results. If a talent for speaking, indispensable to anyone placed at the head of a congregation, had been added to the admirable qualities he displayed in aiding the sick and wounded, to his devotion to the spirit of self-sacrifice, of which he gave many proofs by consecrating his night's rest to them, and by stripping himself of most of his clothes and linen in their behalf, Mr. Van Gogh would certainly have been an accomplished evangelist.
>
> Undoubtedly it would be unreasonable to demand extraordinary talents. But it is evident that the absence of certain qualities may render the exercise of an evangelist's principal function wholly impossible.
>
> Unfortunately this is the case with Mr. Van Gogh. Therefore, the probationary period—some months—having expired, it has been necessary to abandon the idea of retaining him any longer.[4]

It seems that in the eyes of his superiors his inability to preach the Word of God in the formal, organized, ceremonial manner of the church was the deciding factor. This was perhaps a man literally seeking to embody the life of Christ, sacrificing his own needs, but unable to do it in an approved manner within the established religious system. His radical attempt to follow Christ's example led to the church's removal of his ministry.

His letter to his brother Theo in July 1880 expresses his heart:

> You should know that it is the same with evangelists as it is with artists. There is an old academic school, often odious and tyrannical, the "abomination of desolation," in short, men who dress, as it were, in a suit of steel armor, a cuirass, of prejudice and convention. When they are in charge, it is they who hand out the jobs and try, with much red tape, to keep them for their protégés and to exclude the man with an open mind.
>
> Their God is like the God of Shakespeare's drunken Falstaff, "the inside of a church."[5]

In the letter he goes on to indicate that the church leaders are spiritually blind and that his dismissal from the ministry was, "quite simply that my ideas differ from those of the gentlemen who hand out the jobs to individuals who think as they do. It is not just a question of my appearance, which is what they have sanctimoniously reproached me with. It goes deeper, I do assure you."[6]

Nevertheless, his lifestyle of poverty and radical commitment to imitate Christ made him enemies among the religious authorities. The church leaders accused him of "undermining the dignity of the priesthood." For a time later, Vincent continued to work in Wasmes without official position or pay, living in poverty, nursing the victims of a mining disaster, and giving away whatever food and clothing came his way. He left the post on foot, wandered for a while, and ended up back home with his already frustrated parents. His father believed that his son should ultimately be committed to a lunatic asylum.

After this series of failed ministry endeavors, Vincent started painting at age twenty-seven.

While suffering from a number of mental and physical maladies over his lifetime, including severe depression and migraines, Vincent Van Gogh was somehow able to channel those ailments into the creation of his art. Perhaps he used self-righteous anger toward the church to help neutralize depression. He seems to have worked through depression with a hyperactive, hypersensitive state, similar in some ways to the manic phase of bipolar disorder.

He converted his nonfunctioning misery of depression into "active" suffering and developed alternative ways of being in relationship with others. Art experts have suggested that the "impressionistic" style that he became known for was a result of his actual vision of the world. The fluid, swirling colors and halos with which he painted were an outworking of his hyperactive and migraine-pained mind.

In a decade, he created about 2,100 artworks, including approximately 860 oil paintings, most of which date from the last two years of his life. Van Gogh sold only a single painting in his lifetime and died by suspected suicide (although there is debate about whether it was suicide or murder). Posthumously he became one of the most famous and influential figures in the history of Western art. His paintings have sold as the highest priced pieces of art ever. In 1990 one of his paintings sold for $82.5 million at auction. Today he's almost universally regarded as one of the finest painters of all time, although at the end of his own short life he died in anguish and misery.

One of Van Gogh's most universally recognized paintings, now regarded by many as his magnum opus, is *The Starry Night*. He painted it in June 1889 from the east-facing window of his asylum room at Saint-Rémy-de-Provence. He painted the contours of the landscape from the view in his window, but he used his superpower to add an imaginary village.

Interestingly, every light in each house is on, but the little church chapel remains a place of darkness.

The Starry Night is one of the most recognized paintings in Western art and perhaps expresses the view of emerging generations about the church today: the light of Christ no longer shines there. The massive swell of people who now consider themselves "spiritual but not religious" are pushing specifically against a church in which someone can be too radically Christian to be a minister.

Van Gogh's life and work became the fascination of Henri Nouwen. Nouwen, deeply inspired by Van Gogh, also felt at times that his heart for the marginalized and oppressed was at odds with his position as a priest. The "Christ of the coal mines" embodied a ministry that was considered "shepherd malpractice." His work among the poor disabled him from properly serving a congregation. I find that many in ministry have had this kind of experience. Perhaps the state of the church is not dissimilar in many contexts today. Sadly, it seems today that one can be *too Christian* to be a clergyperson, and sometimes the light of Christ seems to shine in every space in the community except the church.

I realize that for some this is a jaded assessment. Reminder, it was my experience of a healing community that was accessible, safe, and real, that changed the trajectory of my life. It was that church community to which I returned when I had come to the end of my rope. I believe the church is a massive force for good all over the world. I'm actually more hopeful for the church than ever before. It's true that I'm critical of a certain version of the church that is known for rigid institutionalism, a version of the church that has lost its missional essence and suffers from apostolic amnesia. That version of the church is passing away, but in its place, there is the groundswell of a movement forming in the fields. In the ashes of the pandemic, we have been given a gift. We have been forced to take a good hard look at what the church is and why it's been in decline for decades.

Right now, we have a massive opportunity to follow the *archegos* and recover a posture of shepherd *malpractice*.

My life has been deeply shaped by three stories Jesus tells in Luke 15, delivered before an audience that consisted of primarily two groups of people, "tax collectors and sinners," who were drawing near, and "Pharisees and the scribes," who were grumbling about the questionable company Jesus kept (vv. 1–2 NRSV). To this mixed crowd Jesus shared three stories that each have a similar structure, theme, and key point.

Each story's structure can be summarized as follows:

1. Something of great value is lost.

2. What's lost is relentlessly sought after and found.

3. When what was lost is recovered, there is a party.

The first story is about a lost sheep, the second about a lost coin, and the third about a lost person. The good shepherd goes after the lost sheep and finds it, and there is a celebration. A woman loses a valuable coin, gets down on her hands and knees until she finds it, then invites over her friends for a party. A lost son squanders everything his father has given him as an inheritance, but "while he [is] still far off," the father sees him; runs to him (inappropriate for Jewish males); recovers him with robe, ring, and sandals; then fires up the grill and throws a house party. Or as Brennan Manning writes of this last story, the father embodies "grace that hikes up the robe and runs breakneck toward the prodigal reeking of sin and wraps him up and decides to throw a party, no ifs, ands, or buts."[7]

Jesus further elaborates his point on this final story by describing the dissatisfaction of an older brother, one who never got lost but faithfully served the father all along. He refused to take part in the party.

Between the two groups of people, unclean sinners and religious leaders, Jesus is making a glaringly obvious point. He has come to seek and save the lost, and rather than grumbling, the religious leaders should be joining both the search party and the afterparty. But like the older brother, they were rejecting the invite to the barbecue.

Let's go a bit deeper with the first story about a lost sheep and a good shepherd. The story can become so familiar to long-term Christians that we miss the controversial nature of what Jesus is saying.

No good shepherd in his right mind would ever leave ninety-nine faithful sheep to the dangers of the wilderness and go after a single stray sheep. They could be attacked by predators, stolen by bandits, or scattered even more. The ninety-nine could be harmed or lost while the shepherd is away. At the very least, the shepherd would lead them to safety first, but surely not leave them in the wilderness.

No good shepherd would do that. That is simply *shepherd malpractice.*

Anyone from the shepherd's union who was present that day would give Jesus a massive fine for a terrible story.

Yet Jesus insists that a good shepherd does indeed leave the ninety-nine to go after a lost one.

Not only that, but when he finds it, he lays it on his shoulders, and brings the lost sheep back to the fold. Then he calls all the friends and neighbors, and they have a roaring celebratory party. They celebrate the sheep once lost, now found. Jesus doesn't hide his main point: "Just so, I tell you, there will be more joy in heaven over one sinner who repents than over ninety-nine righteous persons who need no repentance" (Luke 15:7 NRSV).

Jesus is in some way saying, "While you guys are caring for the ninety-nine, grumbling about the sinners and tax collectors who are leaning in, you should be out here with me seeking after the lost ones!"

The stories are indeed a metaphor for the ministry of Jesus. But we can miss the deeper underlying point. Each of the stories describes the essence and character of God. God is a good shepherd who leaves the ninety-nine to go after one. God is like a woman who will stop everything, get down on her hands and knees, and search until she finds you. God is like a running father whose eyes, even when we have committed red-handed mutiny and run as far away as we can, are on the road, watching and waiting for us to come over the hill. And even while we are still a far way off, he will run to embrace us.

I've taken Jesus' teaching as the guide for my vocation as a clergyperson. I've taken up *shepherd malpractice* as an essential posture in ministry, because I believe that's what it means to be a good shepherd.

This posture is not without its challenges. I am an itinerant, ordained elder in The United Methodist Church. This means I am deployed to serve churches across a state, at the determination of my bishop and a cabinet. Each appointment to a local church is taken year by year. Under the direction of God, there are three main players in the decision of whether a pastor gets moved to a new church each year:

1. The local church (do they want to keep the pastor or not?)

2. The pastor himself or herself (does the pastor want to stay or leave?)

3. The bishop and cabinet (do they feel they need the pastor elsewhere?)

The church in the US has been in plummeting decline for more than fifty years. Some posit that the church is riding a wave of energy that crashed decades ago, but that ride is almost come to shore. Many strategies have been set forth to help the church "grow" again. Len Wilson points out that growth itself needs to be examined and returned to its biblical origins. Yet nothing in the last fifty years has proven effective in reversing this decline.[8]

A "social contract" is the implicit agreement among the members of a community or society. From my view as local practitioner of ministry living on the front lines, part of the problem here is the social contract between congregations and their ministers. The professional minister is sent to do the work of ministry, while the congregation receives it. This is a model of ministry in which the pastor is a hired hand, a spiritual butler to the congregation, who receives their pay to provide this work. The formal expectation of a Methodist congregation is that the appointed clergyperson is sent to lead the church in the areas of Word, sacrament, order, and service, meaning, the pastor preaches and teaches, oversees the sacramental life of the church, orders the life of the church, and serves the needs of the community.

Yet this social contract has moved far from the original ideas of the founder of Methodism, John Wesley, who famously said, in so many words, "The world is my parish."[9] The current social contract expects *the parish to be the pastor's world* (more specifically, the parish is the church facility, and serving the overchurched who reside there is the main task). Wesley's primary focus was those who were outside the church. The "social contract" of early Methodism was about reaching, forming, equipping, and unleashing everyday believers to take their place in the mission of God. People awakened in the field and gathered in small group forums to grow in the life of grace, with the expectation that they would become ministers in their own right.

At my ordination service, Bishop Ken Carter said, "The time of the professional minister is over; the time of the missionary pastor has come."[10] Those words set me free and have become a rally cry of my ministry. For me, and many others my age, becoming a "professional minister" is not very appealing. My hope is to be both a *missionary*, someone who is sent to the lost sheep, and a *pastor*, someone whose first calling is to nurture people in love toward healing. While I don't do this perfectly, I understand this to be my true vocation.

In its original intent, the ministry of the Word—that is, preaching and teaching—is not for the congregation alone, but the larger community. A preacher must also share good news both with those for whom it is *good* and those for whom it is *news* . . . meaning with people who've never heard it before. Further, I see my role as teaching others how to do this, not do it all myself.

Administering the sacraments is also a missional phenomenon. At Wildwood we have welcomed almost three hundred new members in nine years, many by profession of faith, or folks brand-new to the faith. They come to know Jesus through taking communion for the first time and are often baptized into the community. Each week families, including children of every age, receive Holy Communion together in our primary worship experiences. But as a "blended ecology" of church, we also offer Holy Communion in tattoo parlors, at dog parks, in yoga studios, on running tracks, at community centers, in burrito joints, and in digital spaces as we are the church where the church is not.[11]

Many take ordering the life of the church to mean being a kind of manager of the system or a divinely appointed CEO. I gave up my CEO days when I had to sell my business to become a clergyperson, an unfortunate expectation being that most churches can no longer afford to pay their clergy. What if every pastor would start founding companies to make a living like so many others in the gig economy who work multiple jobs?

For me, ordering the life of the church is about ordering the church's life for mission. This includes equipping the laity for ministry, equipping and unleashing them to lead worship, exercise pastoral oversight, and cultivate new Christian communities. Ordering the life of the church is not simply oiling the institutional machinery but joining God's recovery effort to "seek and to save the lost" (Luke 19:10).

Lastly, I serve the people of God to empower them to carry out this mission on the foundation of servanthood. That servanthood is conducted with a particular end in mind. The church, as an extension of Jesus (1 Cor 12:27), is missional by its very nature, a means of grace in itself and a redemptive fellowship. All Christians are called to ministry, as a "priesthood of believers." For me, being an ordained elder means being a servant to believers called to prepare, equip, nourish through sacramental life, and lead in mission.

One of the mentors in my great cloud of witnesses is my seminary professor Dr. Steve Harper. In one of our out-of-the-classroom mentorship sessions, eating slices of pizza in a local dive in downtown Orlando, he told me, "Find the smallest church in your denomination and serve it with all you got."[12] In a church world where so many are climbing the corporate ladder to success, Steve's wisdom has been my guide. Many big, shiny opportunities have been thrown Jill's and my way. Every year we are courted to lead the big, healthy church where the grass is green. But each year our prayer is, "Lord send us to the churches no one else wants or sees." Our special calling is revitalizing congregations. Wildwood has been that community for ten years now.

One of the first things I did upon arrival at Wildwood was take the door off the hinges of my office. I placed it in the sanctuary and preached a sermon series called "The Open Door Policy." I told the "WildOnes" (the name the congregation decided upon) that I would not be in that office. I would visit them, I would hear their stories, I would love them, but that was only part of my job. The larger community was my office. Connecting with people, forming relationships, serving them, this was part of my work too. I was not sent to be a spiritual butler of the congregation. I was sent to be a pastor to a community. The city was my parish, not the congregation only. What I was doing was reversing the social contract.

This did not go over well at several revitalizations. One congregation where I attempted this let me know that this was unacceptable. They had a meeting and voted, frankly, not to grow. My job was to take care of them and preserve their way of doing church; if not, I could hit the road. And hit the road I did after one year.

Just like in a recovery process, if a dying congregation does not have the "gift of desperation," it is unlikely they will be willing to undertake the journey of death and resurrection.

I have been involved with several revitalizations now, congregations who were in a conversation about closure but experienced resurrection. The key to each one was "shepherd malpractice." My focus is not the ninety-nine. My focus is the lost one. At each congregation where I've been sent, there are a couple of willing sheep who want to join the search party. We go searching after lost ones together. This turns worship into a block party. Our worship services are not about caring for already-Christians who've heard the good news their whole lives and never shared it. Instead, worship is an experience of equipping missionaries.

This is not an easy posture to take. As Pastor Dan once taught me, "Sheep bite, and sometimes they shit in your office."

At Wildwood, a group of key leaders who had attended the church most of their lives decided it was time for me to go. They could no longer tolerate my shepherd malpractice. These are people I greatly loved and respected. I spent time in their homes and beside their hospital beds. I baptized their grandbabies.

They organized a meeting to send me packing. One of my key supporters started off, "Pastor Michael, your first sermon was called the 'Arranged Marriage.' You told us that you were here to be our pastor until we wanted a divorce. Well, the time has come. We want a divorce." They went around the circle one by one, each taking a turn to tell me why it was time for me to leave. It felt as if each one stepped forward to plunge a knife into my heart.

Then came one sweet ninety-seven-year-old man whom I loved and cherished. He looked me in the eyes and said these words, "Michael you are too much like Jesus to be our pastor. Jesus didn't have a church to take care of; you do." That's what he said, word for word. It's in the meeting minutes. How does a person who loves God and who has gone to church his whole life somehow get to the place where his clergyperson can be "too much like Jesus"? How can there be such a disconnect between what Jesus was doing, equipping a small group of people to be shepherds, priests, and healers, in their own right, and what the church is today?

Frederick Buechner says, "The place God calls you to is the place where your deep gladness and the world's deep hunger meet."[13] My deep hunger is not to spend my time cleaning up sheep shit or healing from their bites. My deep hunger is to teach the whole people of God how to chase down lost sheep. Because inside me, there is a lost sheep, the one Jesus came to get from the floor of a solitary confinement cell, a lost sheep who even today wanders away from the flock.

To do anything else would be deep hypocrisy for me. It would be a violation of my vocation. This would simply become a new form of the "impostor" syndrome. Sure, I could hide away in the armor of professionalism, but I would be betraying my wounded Healer, Jesus. *It would be hiding my wounds, not pulling off the bandages with others, so we can find healing together.*

I suspect I'm not the only one who feels this way. Perhaps not all of us are called to a ministry with lost sheep. But we all must know in the depths of our being exactly *who* and *what* we are called to. Jesus confronted the religious leadership of his day because of their hypocrisy (Matt 3:7). They projected one thing but were in fact something different on the inside (Matt 23:27). The routine of religiosity and the obsession with ritual purity had become more important than the people they were called to shepherd (Mark 3:1–5). He described their eye condition, calling them "blind guides" (Matt 15:14; 23:16, 24). But their eye condition was connected to a fatal heart condition, "hardness of heart" (Mark 3:5; 10:5 NRSV). Their rigid, hard-eyed surety of knowing led them to accuse Jesus of hanging out with sketchy, unclean people and to dismiss his miracles as fraudulent.

This is a warning for all of us to check our own hearts. Western church culture worships at the altar of effectiveness, efficiency, and successfully growing "mega" congregations. If a leader is effective, we might overlook that they are mean, abusive, or controlling. The character of leaders seems secondary to their ability to "grow" a church. We are watching what seems like a never-ending parade of one "high profile" fallen leader after another.

The *missio Dei* (mission of God) has been hijacked in the church growth conversation. We cannot overlook that a missional church flows from the loving heart of God. Its origin is the compassion of God. Overemphasis on orthodoxy (ὀρθοδοξία *orthos* "right" *doxía* "opinion") or even (ὀρθοπραξία *orthos* "right" *praxy* "practice"), while disregarding orthopathy (ὀρθός *orthos* "right" and πάθος *pathos* "suffering"), fails the Jesus test at every level.

In the 1970s Wesleyan and Pentecostal theologians introduced the term "orthopathy," to describe that a "right experience" of God was just as essential as right belief and practice. For instance, the religious leaders who conflicted with Jesus were orthodox in their belief and practice. But they did not represent the heart of God. Thus, their heart condition… hardness of heart.

The *passio Dei* (the passion of God), is embodied in the incarnation of Jesus. More specifically, the suffering, crucifixion, and death of Jesus (i.e. the passion) ultimately reveals the heart, nature, and power of God like nothing else in creation. When we see Jesus on the cross, we see the heart of the Good Shepherd. God's nature is the self-emptying, other-oriented, and sacrificial love fully displayed in the crucifixion. The passion of Christ expresses God's immersion and connection to human vulnerability and suffering.

On the cross, God shows us that his weakness is his superpower.

We are an Eden people on a journey toward recovering our innate "very goodness." But we cannot rightly emphasize sanctification being re-conformed to the *Imago Dei* (the image of God) the ultimate end of the *Missio Dei* (the mission of God) without doing so in the nature and character of the *Passio Dei* (the passion of God). The *Missio Dei* (divine act of sending and mission) and the *Passio Dei* (divine act of compassionate being-with and incarnate interpenetration) are streams flowing in the same river of life. The mission of God is grounded in God's essence as compassionate caregiver.

We are all in danger of defaulting back to the impostor. Religious hypocrisy is the most death-dealing form of the impostor syndrome. It stems from a diminished way of seeing others. We harden our hearts to those we consider "unclean." But when the church becomes known as a place of harm rather than healing, we have lost the heart of the Good Shepherd, he who kept "sinners and tax collectors" as his constant company. The only logical result of good "shepherd malpractice" leads to a church in the wilderness where the lost sheep live, a church in the wild.

15

A CHURCH IN THE WILD

I am about to do a new thing;
now it springs forth, do you not perceive it?
I will make a way in the wilderness
and rivers in the desert.
The wild animals will honor me,
the jackals and the ostriches;
for I give water in the wilderness,
rivers in the desert,
to give drink to my chosen people,
the people whom I formed for myself
so that they might declare my praise.
Isaiah 43:19–21

Two of our greatest twenty-first-century poets, JAY-Z and Kanye West, have said there's "no church in the wild" in their song by that name. It's possible that they are correct. One dimension of their poem is taking a shot at the hypocrisy of the church, mentioning "lies on the lips of the priest."[1] We can't argue with them there. Yet at the heart of their poem is another idea. In the dark world of drug dealing, the church not only has no relevance, but no presence period. So, in the carnage of the streets, one makes one's own god . . . and it's you.

We need a church in the wild.

For better or for worse, God's plan for the healing of the world is the church. This community is somehow mysteriously the continuing incarnation of Jesus' body in the earth. A community of fallible human beings, gathered around the risen Jesus, empowered by the Spirit, who derive their life from the life of God. Jesus said he would "build" his church, and nothing in or under the world could stop it (Matt 16:18).

Jesus, the *archegos* who was accused of shepherd malpractice by his critics, founded a church in the wild, among the wild ones, a church outside the bounds of the religious systems of the day. Jesus planted his church in the wild. He's calling those who want to paint with ashes to do the same.

Throughout history, there have been Christians who have followed Jesus' lead. They were able to take the throwaways, the marginalized, and the wounded and create beautiful things. Consider this: In the 1740s, French philosopher and composer Jean-Jacques Rousseau came to visit Venice, Italy. While overall quite critical of Italian music, he had journeyed to Venice to experience the legendary *figlie del coro* (the "daughters of the choir"). This all-female group of musicians was led by a Venetian composer named Antonio Vivaldi. Vivaldi, also known as the Red Priest for his bright-red hair, was an Italian Baroque composer, virtuoso violinist, teacher, impresario, and Roman Catholic priest. The figlie del coro was the primary group of musicians who played his compositions. He cross-trained many of them to play multiple instruments: violins, oboes, violas, harpsichords, French horns, and double basses. In their live performances they would frequently change instruments as they played.

Rousseau was frustrated on his visit because he could not actually *see* the women perform. Hanging between the church balconies where they played was a curtain that obscured them. Only their dimly lit swaying silhouettes could be seen through the thin veil as they performed. Rousseau became obsessed with seeing these "daughters of the choir" with his own eyes. Finally, a patron granted his wish.

The patron arranged for Rousseau to meet the girls in a salon. He was shocked at what he saw. This choir of female prodigies both young and old was "horrid" to behold. Some of the girls were missing an eye, fingers, a foot, or an entire limb. Others were badly disfigured by smallpox, syphilis, and other venereal diseases they contracted at birth. The female choir was the result of the Venice underworld's sex industry. Many female newborns were simply dumped in the canals and back alleys, left to die.

The *Ospedale della Pietà*, or "Hospital of Pity," was a response to this plight. Babies could be dropped in the *scafetta*, a drawer built into the outer wall of the Ospedale. If a child could be fit inside that drawer, the Ospedale would raise them. While the Ospedale was a public-private partnership, overseen by volunteer boards of wealthy Venetians, daily life inside the institution functioned very much like a Christian monastery. Girls were trained to play musical instruments to perform in nearby churches. By the eighteenth century their music had become a financial engine not only to support the social welfare system but to attract tourists. Eventually the orphaned daughters of the Venetian sex industry became the first international rock stars.[2]

The Ospedale commissioned composers to produce original works, and Vivaldi wrote 140 concertos specifically for the *Pieta*. Vivaldi had health complications throughout his lifetime. In particular, he suffered from asthma. In spite of his lifelong health challenges, Vivaldi learned to play the violin, compose, and engage in other strenuous musical activities, including playing wind instruments. At the age of fifteen, he began studying to become a priest and was ordained in 1703 at the age of 25.

"The Red Priest" became *maestro di violino* (master of violin) at the Ospedale della Pietà in September 1703. For three decades, he composed most of his major works while appointed there, with his chief musicians being the figlie del coro. He was the primary instructor for the girls' musical education, and he trained many of the most talented members of the Ospedale's renowned orchestra and choir. Vivaldi wrote his concertos, cantatas, and sacred vocal music specifically for these orphans to play.

Nevertheless, the board of directors of the Ospedale were less than enthusiastic with Vivaldi's performances. Each year he lived with the possibility of the board voting to dismiss him as a teacher, much as an itinerant Methodist clergyperson can do fruitful work in the community yet be considered ineffective in caring for the existing congregation. Vivaldi was proficient in shepherd malpractice. In 1709, the board voted to dismiss him with a 7–6 vote. Can you imagine being part of the board that decided to dismiss one of the most widely popular composers in history?

During his year of dismissal from the Ospedale, Vivaldi traveled as a freelance musician. The board became painfully aware of Vivaldi's gifts and impact in his absence. In 1711 they voted unanimously to bring him back, but now with more responsibilities. By 1716 he was appointed as *maestro de' concerti* (music director), responsible for all of the institution's musical activity.[3]

Not only was Vivaldi able to nurture and train orphans to produce some of the most beautiful symphonies ever created, but he innovated within an institutional system. Cultivating church in the wild, on the dark edges of human civilization with the throwaways does not mean one must abandon more monolithic systems. This activity can actually bring renewal to those organizations.

Vivaldi used the brokenness around him to make music that healed the world. He painted with ashes.

<hr />

If there is to be a church in the wild, what would it look like?

We are sitting cross-legged in a circle on the floor of the tattoo parlor. You can hear the buzz of tattoo guns humming in the background behind the ballad of the Dropkick Murphys playing on the shop speakers. There is chatter from patrons talking to artists about their dreams for a piece. Others are scheduling their piercings and signing the paperwork.

The group in the circle is an eclectic bunch, mostly Gen Z and millennials, with a smattering of Gen Xers. Starbucks cups, water bottles, and Bibles litter the coffee table. They encircle a clay chalice (this one from Assisi) and a Hawaiian bread loaf from Publix. Amid the noise and the chatter, this circle of friends is engrossed in a deep discussion.

Each person around the circle is sharing his or her "tattoo story." Individuals show the art engraved in their flesh and talk about the meaning behind the symbolism and what led to their decision to permanently etch it into their flesh. Mostly we only showcase appropriate locations on the body, although occasional breasts, pubic areas, and ass cheeks have been showcased in the past.

Every tattoo has a unique and significant story. It is a vulnerable moment of soul baring by that individual. Of course, many of us have drunkalogues about waking up in a vomiting hangover and discovering we'd added a new artistic addition to our flesh, a heart that says "mom," an anchor, or a poop emoji (I've seen them all). But besides those anomalies, there is a deep and powerful memory connected to each tattoo.

For example, one twentysomething had tattooed "*imago dei*" in rainbow letters over the scars on her wrist. She took the handwriting from her deceased mother's letters and incorporated them into the piece. "I want to think about how much my momma loved me next time I'm trying to kill myself like a dumbass," she laughs.

Adam talks about his first gang tattoo, the badge of honor he received after getting beat up. "I'm ready to cover it over with a scroll with my favorite Bible verse, though," he said.

Meghan shares about her golden retriever, her furry companion for over fifteen years. Nicole, a sleeved forty-two-year-old, talks about her hummingbird, a memorial to a childhood friend: "The morning of her funeral, there was a tiny hummingbird flittering from flower to flower. I knew that was her." The memory still brings her to tears.

Melanie has her deceased son's handwriting on her forearm, it reads, "I love you, Mom." She says, "These were the last words he said to me in a letter he wrote one week before he overdosed on fentanyl."

As each person shares about his or her tattoos, the individual is also sharing about his or her pain, hopes, and dreams. Ironically, the entire group is also doing theology. Instinctually they share about how they each felt God was with them in that significant moment, or maybe not with them. They are unwrapping their wounds before the group, showing each other their broken places.

I try to pull all the strands of those stories together and share a moment from the life of Jesus, how he was present with people in their moments of celebration, like a wedding party, where someone dropped the ball on keeping the wine flowing. Or how he wept with others at the funeral. How he touched the unclean and the untouchables, whom others went out of their way to avoid. We reflect on that together. People ask questions, make comments, and contribute what that story means to them.

Then we all huddle up around that messy coffee table. I pour the grape juice into the chalice and take the bread loaf out of the bag. We reflect for a moment on how messy the table was where those first disciples gathered and how they too were ordinary broken people, people who made mistakes, had a few too many, and did weird sexual things. But these were people whom Jesus called friends, siblings, and beloved.

We become aware that Jesus is there with us, embracing us as we are, not as we should be, inviting us to reflect on our wounds as we gather around him, the wounded One, whose blood is in the cup, whose body is the bread. Somehow, right there in the tattoo parlor, we commune with the wounded One, and as we do, we find a moment of healing. A moment of wholeness. A moment of shalom. Our world is at peace.

In that space, people acknowledge their brokenness and pain. They learn about a God of unconditional love and then *commune* with that God—many for the first time.

From an Africentric perspective this is communal healing. In Western schools of therapy, the highly trained and well compensated expert guides the client toward individuation, self-realization, and a well developed ego. However, African therapeutic modalities include testimony therapy, which focuses on sharing in a collective story.

Testimony therapy is communitarian and social constructionist in nature. Ubuntu—if we are persons through other persons our healing will most powerfully manifest in community with others.

For example, in the black church testify'n is a ritual in which members of the community "share their testimony." The narrative includes an honest articulation of some struggle or pain, followed by the pivot often captured by the words "but God…" It was hard, *but God* brought me through. I went through a struggle, *but God* was faithful. The community participates through call and response in the individual's story with "go ahead" "tell it" "make it plain" and "amen."[4]

This is a therapeutic process that brings healing to individuals in the context of community. It is a resource for marginalized and oppressed people who are denied access to some of the more exclusive (and expensive) Western healing modalities employed by individualistic cultures. Communal healing of individual and collective trauma is closely aligned with the collectivistic culture of the Hebrew people and the tradition of lament.

Tattoo Parlor Church is one of the many "fresh expressions of church" with which I am involved.[5] A Fresh Expression is simply a form of church for our changing culture established primarily for the benefit of people who are not yet members of any church. If the church is Jesus' plan for the healing of the world, the most innovative, important, and restorative thing we can possibly do is cultivate new forms of church with people who don't go to church. As someone who lived seasons far from the church, I have a passion to find ways to form community with the people who still live in that faraway land.

These contextual churches are little communities where the four healing questions from testimony therapy are our guide:

1. What happened to you?

2. How does what happened to you affect you now?

3. What do you need to heal?

4. In spite of what happened to you, what gives you strength to go on?

Again, my experience of the church as being a healing community that was accessible, safe, and real changed the trajectory of my life. Now I have given myself to cultivating those kinds of communities for others. The challenge is that many people find the church unappealing, for several reasons:

- It is *inaccessible*. It is not close, not contextual, it meets at a less-than-ideal time, and it speaks a language they don't understand.

- It is *unsafe*. It is seen as not inclusive, as an atmosphere of judgment rather than grace, and as a place of harm rather than healing.

- It is *unreal*. The pastor and the people seem less than genuine; there is a lack of honesty about real wounds, and therefore real healing is not taking place.

Healing requires vulnerability in an atmosphere of grace.

People need a safe community where they can take the bandages off their wounds. The healing process requires us to appropriately grieve our losses and come to terms with our trauma. This necessitates us being real . . . articulating our grieving in an uncensored way. This is why many people report that 12-step fellowships are more transformative than church communities. Recovery meetings provide perhaps the clearest example of testimony therapy... and it only costs one dollar in the basket.

My friends sitting in the circle at AA and saying, "This fucking sucks" are doing in a modern way what the psalmist was doing in the lament psalms. Sometimes the anger is aimed at God, and that's okay. We can beat our fists on God's chest until we can't lift our arms anymore. God can take it! We can lie on God's lap and cry ourselves to sleep, God will be there when we wake up. This kind of healing takes place most powerfully in community

A church always singing doxology and never lament is not being real. Loss and pain require an appropriate period of grieving. A church rushing "back to normal" amid a pandemic with a long tail is unhealthy. We are inadvertently minimizing people's loss and grief, diminishing their capacity to heal.

The psalms teach us how to paint with ashes. Lament psalms are a resource for communal healing. They give us a vehicle to articulate our emotions to God in an honest way.

> My God, my God, why have you forsaken me?
> Why are you so far from saving me,
> so far from my cries of anguish?
> My God, I cry out by day, but you do not answer,
> by night, but I find no rest." (Ps 22:1–2)

> In your unfailing love, silence my enemies;
> destroy all my foes,
> for I am your servant. (Ps 143:12)

> Blessed is he who seizes your infants and dashes them against the rocks. (Ps 137:9 BSB)

The language of lament is not neat and clean. It is raw, primitive, and real. It is an honest expression of the language of grief. If we hold on to these emotions, they keep us sick and stuck. A community that is accessible, safe, and real can give people space to express their struggles and find healing.

Emerging generations are rarely finding congregations that embody this kind of community, and for the vast majority church has simply become inaccessible. Many people will never walk into our sanctuary on Sunday mornings no matter how amazing worship might be. So, we must form these healing communities in the spaces and rhythms where people do life, around the practices that already connect them there. They become like little islands of new creation dotting the landscape of our communities.

This includes taking seriously how new Christian communities can form in digital space as well. Our team has cultivated multiple online fresh expressions with people who have no relationship with a traditional congregation:

- Supper Table Church: a group of parents who prepare themed meals, pop up a screen at the table, and connect with others to pray, discuss a Jesus story, and share wisdom on homeschooling their children.

- Create: a community of artists who gather in a Zoom room for a devotional, prayer, and a time of artistic expression, including paintings, poetry, and crafts.

- Living Room Church: a community designed to support and celebrate the spiritual growth of its fourteen hundred group members: "A safe zone to connect, discuss real issues, and heal with other imperfect people. A space to reflect on Scripture, worship, learn, and pray together. A church that's open 24/7, providing relationships and spiritual resources. Located where you hang out every day already . . . Facebook!"6

- Yoga Church Digital: a community of people who gather in the safety of their own homes for a devotional, prayer time, and guided yoga practice.

Using the stories of Luke 15, church in the wild would be like a community planted for all the lost sheep who ran off. But rather than bringing them back to the fold, it would be like creating a whole new community of lost sheep where they live, away from the ninety-nine. It is like planting a church in the pig trough where the lost son went to squander his inheritance. Not only does the father run to the son while he is "still a long way off" (v. 20); he builds a new house in that foreign land.

These little new Christian communities are spread across a whole area of north central Florida. Not only do we meet in the many diverse places I listed earlier (the dog park, burrito joints, etc.) but in Facebook groups and Zoom rooms. They are places where people are learning to paint with ashes.

One of these communities was called Trap Stars for Jesus. As we gathered in the Martin Luther King Jr. building for pancake breakfasts, games for kids, and Jesus stories, we began to connect with the drug dealers hustling on the corner in front of the building.

They came over to join us for breakfast, talk, and share stories. My friend Eric Wilkins and I invited them to come over and talk about how to start legitimate businesses, how to use their God-given entrepreneurial impulses in a legal way to create wealth. They could lift their families out of poverty and a culture of systemic racism, rather than ending up dead or in prison.

Eric was convicted of murder and spent most of his young life in prison. Today he is my co-pastor. As Eric and I are both reformed drug dealers turned pastors, we can understand their pain and speak their language. We help them get business licenses, purchase equipment, and secure insurance and worker's compensation policies to start their companies.

This is what a church in the wild looks like.

Now, of course, with a network of fifteen fresh expressions across an area, the traditional hierarchical model of leadership doesn't work. It requires a shared leadership approach. The professional pastor model is a no go in the wild. The Methodists have a tradition of the circuit rider, a clergyperson who travels a circuit, serving a network of churches across a region. In between the traveling ministers' visits, the work of ministry was led and sustained by the people.

Every person has a wicked problem, an issue that is complex and resistant to resolution because of incomplete, contradictory, and changing requirements that are often difficult to recognize. This is where our own experience and passions are brought to bear on some fragmentation in the world that breaks our hearts.

My wicked problem is the clergy caste system. There is usually nowhere in the world that I feel more out of place than at clergy gatherings or faculty meetings at the seminary. Some of my colleagues have never had a speeding ticket, much less multiple felonies. Because of my unique life experience and calling, I am often minimized, hidden, and not granted a seat at the tables where decisions are made.

I have felt like an outsider in the very denomination that nurtured me and gave me life. In the clergy caste system, we are not evaluated by our faithfulness and fruitfulness, but rather by whom we know, our pedigrees, and our willingness to brownnose our way up the hierarchy. In this system, only the most politically savvy leaders are granted seats at the inner circle of power, which they hold on to at all costs.

In this system, the laity are a kind of secondhand citizens. Whether this is spoken or just part of clergy caste culture, laity are seen as "less than" and incompetent to be ministers in their own right. We pay lip service to the idea of "lay-led ministries" but the system itself actually suppresses the gifts of laity.

There is no biblical argument for a distinction between laity and clergy. The church Jesus designed is one in which we are a "priesthood of all believers"[7] (see 1 Peter 2:5–9). Every Christian is ordained in the waters of baptism to serve as an apostle, prophet, evangelist, shepherd, or teacher (see Eph 4:1–16). While some are given the gift of leadership, the clergy laity hierarchy is not what the Bible portrays.

Jesus was, institutionally speaking, a layperson. The son of a carpenter, and although trained in the rabbinic tradition, he was likely not of the priestly caste. The disciples he chose, while some were theologically trained, were not priests either. They were everyday people, fishermen, tax collectors, female entrepreneurs, and tentmakers. Some were "sinners," and prostitutes too. Most of them were only teenagers when they left everything to follow Jesus. He cultivated his church outside the religious system of his day. He planted a church in the wild with the people who lived outside of convention.

Jesus didn't do the ministry to or for them. He taught them how to do what he was doing. He sent them to cast out demons, heal the sick, and proclaim the kingdom. When the hungry crowds were pressing in, he said to his followers, "You give them something to eat" (Mark 6:37). Jesus' "discipleship program" was on-the-job training, not studying religious texts back at the church compound or seminary. He took these ordinary people and turned them into priests to their own social spheres. Jesus' goal was building disciples who would do greater things than he did (John 14:12).

Korehira Watanabe is one of Japan's last remaining swordsmiths. Watanabe has honed his craft for forty years while attempting to recreate the mythical Koto sword and admits only occasionally that he has been able to do so. Watanabe was disowned by his family when he chose the path of swordsmith. He argues that modern shortcuts have caused the tradition of sword making to wear thin over time. Watanabe believes that a master does not just pass on the technique of sword making to a disciple, but also his heart and passion for the tradition. He says it is his goal to build a better disciple than he is. He wants his disciple to surpass him as a sword maker. Perhaps Watanabe knows more about discipling than most of us pastors.[8]

The greatest artists create communities of students.

Those who become master painters of ashes learn to build communities of apprentices. They create a studio space where people can explore their gifts and develop their skills. Apprenticeship is on-the-job training. The master models the behavior he or she hopes to see in apprentices and teaches them how to refine their abilities.

The traditional institutional church paradigm trains clergy to grow fruit on their own trees. This fruit is measured by the metrics of nickels and noses, how much money and how many people. A pastor is successful if he or she can grow the numbers. We can say that a minister is fruitful—just look: all the numbers are up and to the right. Clergy who want to keep their jobs in this system must make themselves indispensable. We become the professional producers of religious goods and services, and our people become consumers.

The first ten years of my ministry I was passionate about growing fruit on my own tree. I loved when people said, "What a great sermon," or, "That book changed my life," or "Your visit meant so much to me." I wanted people to stop and notice my tree and say, "Look at all that fruit!"

Now, I want to spend the rest of my ministry growing fruit on other people's trees.

Painting with ashes is deeply about fruit growing through others. We have to give up the temptation to be noticed, to play institutional games, and to shout "Look at me!" This can't be measured by most conventional church metrics. When you are growing fruit on other people's trees, others may not even recognize that you are doing it.

In fact, a healthy church in the wild might need a new set of metrics entirely. It might not look very healthy on paper at all.

What if healthy churches don't need full-time appointed clergy because the people own the ministry themselves? What if they don't need paid staff because the mission is sustained by devoted people who work everyday jobs in the gig economy? What if they have very little overhead and dedicate most or all of their tithes toward meeting human need in their communities? What if the local church can be the seminary, so Christian leaders don't need lots of debt or degrees to be effective?

The Red Priest of Venice took society's casualties, the ones no one else wanted or even saw, and turned them into musical geniuses. The street orphans whom no one had any hope for became the rock stars of the orchestral world. What a fitting image for a church in the wild, a church where God can take a ragtag group of throwaways, the discarded and the down and out, and turn them into wounded healers, whose music could heal the world.

A church in the wild will need to be in some ways . . . wild, as in not sculpted or domesticated. It needs to spring up from the context in an appropriate way. It can still be in relationship with and even give life to the inherited church, but each needs to be free to grow in its own way. I have given my life to the inherited church, but I refuse to accept its confines. The world is my church. The wild is my church. My congregation is the dope boys, the tricks, the strippers, and the junkies. I am the pastor of the WildOnes.

In July 2020, in the middle of a pandemic, Jill and I were sent back to become the pastors of that little church that pulled me out of the gutter, St. Mark's United Methodist Church in Ocala, Florida. The church is fragile, on death's door, really. Worship attendance has dwindled. There are not enough tithes coming in to pay the bills. Yet a handful of the people who were present at my infant baptism, watched me run around breaking things, and fed me through their never-ending potlucks are still there. They prayed with my grandmother after bullets had whistled inches away from her back. I now stand in the sanctuary where grace-filled waters trickled across the top of my infant head to preach the Word.

St. Mark's is a church in the wild. Today, we house a homeless shelter in our facility, called Open Arms Village, where men re-entering society after incarceration can find shelter and a 7 × 77th chance. Those men find jobs, get a driver's license for the first time, and enroll in college there. We have weekly food distributions and a drive-through community dinner. There are two sober houses on our property, where people who want recovery can live in community with others. Additionally, we have a dedicated AA building and a dedicated NA (Narcotics Anonymous) building. Every day, multiple times a day, they hold recovery meetings where people can find a kind space to heal from their wounds. I got clean and sober in those rooms. I found the G.O.D. (gift of desperation) and learned the design for living there. To me this is a thin space, holy ground, where Jesus seems to be busy 24/7.

There on that holy ground, we regularly find syringes, empty dope bags, and broken beer bottles. People experiencing homelessness sleep under the breezeway, because they know we won't call the cops. Occasionally we even catch people having sex in one of the recovery buildings or doing a drug deal in the parking lot. It's messy, but this is what a church in the wild looks like.

Every once in a while, one of my students finally gets out of jail and comes to knock on my office door. They tell me they think Jesus might have saved their soul, and I tell them how wonderful that is, but now AA will save their ass, so meet me at the nooner tomorrow. We go over to the sanctuary, the same place where Dan and I stood the day I got out of jail, and we pray together. Those are the blessed ones, the ones who find their way to the holy ground, the WildOnes, who find a home at the church in the wild.

Unfortunately, many never find their way.

On September 27, 2018, my little brother, McKinley, died in my arms from a drug overdose. He had just finished a ten-year prison sentence for telling a clerk in a jiffy store to give him the money in the drawer when he was a youth. Because we were born in poverty and had no ability to acquire proper legal defense, McKinley was given the maximum possible sentence for his crime, a crime for which I've seen wealthy white kids get off on probation. The prison system deformed my little brother's soul even further than the streets did.

He spent almost half of his young life incarcerated. When he was released, I had a place for him to live and a job. He decided to go back to old friends and family members. Within a month, he had relapsed back into intravenous drug use. Within two months, he was dead at thirty four years old.

I was in the middle of a speaking engagement when the hospital called me. They told me I needed to come quickly, as they weren't sure how much longer he would live. When he overdosed, the people he was using drugs with simply left him lying in the trap where they were getting high together. By the time he was found, his brain was irreparably damaged and most of his organs had shut down.

I agonized over my little brother in prayer for four days. At his bedside, holding his bloated yellow hand, I had a vision. I saw him as a little boy, before the scars, before the tattoos, and before the pain and trauma. Jesus took him by the hand, smiled back at me, and they went smiling hand and hand into the garden of new creation.

My little brother died like the thief on the cross beside Jesus. By all accounts, he had lived no life worthy of salvation. But in his unconscious mind, somehow Jesus said to him, "Today you will be with me in paradise" (Luke 23:43). Finally, after coming to terms with the fact that only the machines were keeping him alive, I signed the consent to turn them off. McKinley found his ultimate healing.

As my little brother died in my arms, I had my own flash of memories. He and I as little acolyte boys in the church services our grandma made us go to in the sanctuary where I'm now the pastor. Playing in the rain. Holding each other as my mother was being beaten in the next room. Making trouble together, getting high, and committing crimes. We had the same experience of church as children, but his became a source of resentment, while mine became my only true hope. He could not find healing for his wounds in this life.

My little brother's death is now more ashy paint on my palette. I use it to push through the pain and paint portraits of healing for others, to let them know they don't have to end their story that way.

We continue to live in what the US surgeon general first dubbed "the opioid crisis." The greatest substance abuse epidemic in the history of our country continues. Deaths from the overproduction and overprescription of synthetic opioids continue to kill people in record numbers.[9] The substance changes—morphine, OxyContin, methadone, and today fentanyl—but the core wound is the same.

We know this is a wound that can be healed. And we know a wounded Healer. Recovery groups can be places where people find healing. I believe every single congregation can do something to help. Whether it's repurposing our church facilities to house programs, giving 12-step fellowships space to meet, or starting Christian recovery ministries . . . we can make a difference.

Could there be a church in the wild for people like my little brother? Those with tears tattooed beneath their eyes? Those who jam a needle in their arm to escape their pain and grief? A church where they would find a chorus of others with which to sing the broken hallelujah?

I'm not sure those kinds of churches exist in most communities. But they should exist in every community, and I will give my dying breath to create them. I will cultivate communities in the wild, where people can learn to paint with ashes. Will you join me? Will you use your wounds to heal the broken in your neighborhood? Will you too paint with ashes?

CONCLUSION

A GALLERY IN THE GARDEN: A PARABLE

Then the angel showed me the river of the water of life, bright as crystal, flowing from the throne of God and of the Lamb through the middle of the street of the city. On either side of the river is the tree of life with its twelve kinds of fruit, producing its fruit each month; and the leaves of the tree are for the healing of the nations.
Revelation 22:1–2 NRSV

There is a city with a garden. There in that New Jerusalem is the tree of life and a river that flows from the throne of God. The "leaves of the tree are for the healing of the nations." There is a garden where a weeping world can come find healing. When we touch the leaves, rub them together in our hands, and apply them to each other's wounds, there is healing. There is a healing tree.

In the shade of the tree, I see a gallery, a hall that goes on and on where the fallen tree leaves have been turned into parchment and canvases. Everyone is a child here. We are still covered in the ashes of the world that was before, but we can all run naked in the rain here, catching the drops on our tongues. We laugh as we are washed clean. There is full and final healing here. The children step forward to place their paintings in the hall. The gallery goes on and on, telling the story of every wounded healer who ever lived.

When we stop to glance at each painting, it moves and comes alive. Suddenly we enter into the experience of that person's life. We see what that artist saw. We hear what that artist heard. We feel what that artist felt. While the pain is real and true, it also seems like the prequel to the true story now. Before, we could only see as in a mirror, dimly. We could only know in part. Now we can see the whole picture. Now we can know as we are fully known.

We can see how each one of us was interconnected in a web of humanity, the fullness of *ubuntu*. We can now see that all of us were doing our best to paint with the ashes we were given or even the ones we made. Each person took those raw materials and painted creation with goodness, beauty, and truth. Now, somehow, those very works have become the ingredients of the new creation. We could spend eternity in the gallery, touching each leaf, living through each story.

But there is a healing Gardener in the garden. The wounded Healer, who is "making all things new." Making all things new is not about discarding, destroying, wiping away, or starting over. It's about taking what exists and reconfiguring, reworking, and reshaping what is. Even the pain, even the desperation, is somehow present, but God wipes "every tear from [our] eyes" (Rev 21:4). The tears are still there, the memories, the lives of struggle lived. But when God touches those liquid prayers that flow from our eyes, the sting of death, the pain of grief, is healed. Death becomes the seed of resurrection.

As we touch the open wounds of the wounded One, now, finally, our healing can be complete. Now eternally, the ashes with which we painted will become the ingredients of the new creation. The One who is seated on the throne has made them new.

NOTES

A PARABLE: CHILDREN IN THE ASHES

1 Liam Giliver, "Greta Thunberg on the Cover of TIME: 'Now I Am Speaking to the Whole World'," *Plant Based News*, May 16, 2019, https://plantbasednews. org/news/greta-thunberg-cover-time/; Jonathan Watts, "The Greta Thunberg Effect: At Last, MPs Focus on Climate Change," *Guardian* (UK), April 23, 2019, https://web.archive.org/web/20190828192832/https://www.theguardian.com/ environment/2019/apr/23/greta-thunberg; *Forbes*, "The World's 100 Most Powerful Women," 2020 ranking, https://www.forbes.com/power-women/list/.

2 Greta Thunberg, "School Strike for Climate," December 12, 2018, YouTube video (TEDx Talks), 11:10, https://www.youtube.com/ watch?v=EAmmUIEsN9A&t=106s; Allison Rourke, "Greta Thunberg Responds to Asperger's Critics: 'It's a Superpower'," *Guardian*, September 2, 2019, https://www. theguardian.com/environment/2019/sep/02/greta-thunberg-responds-to-aspergers-critics-its-a-superpower.

3 Michael Ford, *Wounded Prophet: A Portrait of Henri J. M. Nouwen* (New York: Doubleday, 2002), 155.

4 Riaan Van der Merwe, "Broken Wholeness: A Critical Analysis of Henri JM Nouwen's Spirituality of Vulnerability and Its Possible Value for the Current Discourse on Health and Wholeness," *Stellenbosch Theological Journal* 2, no. 2 (2016): 594–95.

5 Henri Nouwen, *Reaching Out: The Three Movements of the Spiritual Life* (Garden City, NY: Image Books, 1986), 11.

6 Van der Merwe, 602–3.

7 Sumitra, "Artist Uses Ashes of the Deceased to Paint Portraits of Them," Oddity Central, February 20, 2014, https://www.odditycentral.com/art/artist-uses-ashes-of-the-deceased-to-paint-portraits-of-them.html.

INTRODUCTION

1 Robert H. Woods and Naaman K. Wood, eds., *Words and Witnesses: Communication Studies in Christian thought from Athanasius to Desmond Tutu* (Peabody, MS: Hendrickson, 2018), 280.

2 Woods and Wood, 282.

3 Woods and Wood, 281.

4 Henri J. Nouwen, *The Wounded Healer: Ministry in Contemporary Society* (Garden City, NY: Doubleday, 1990), xvi.

CHAPTER 1

1 Ross Adam, "Last Survivor of Legendary Warsaw Orphanage Dies in Israel," Aish, February 13, 2021, https://www.aish.com/jw/s/Last-Survivor-of-Legendary-Warsaw-Orphanage-Dies-in-Israel.html.

2 Adam.

3 Joseph Arnon, "Who Was Janusz Korczak?" Jewish Virtual Library, accessed July 8, 2021, https://www.jewishvirtuallibrary.org/jsource/biography/Janusz_Korczak.pdf.

4 Arnon, 24.

5 Donna Brown Agins, *Maya Angelou: A Biography of an Award-Winning Poet and Civil Rights Activist* (Berkeley Heights, NJ: Enslow, 2013), 13.

6 Len Wilson, *Think Like a Five Year Old: Reclaim Your Wonder and Create Great Things* (Nashville: Abingdon Press, 2015).

7 John Wesley, *The Journal of John Wesley* (Chicago: Moody, 1951), 36, http://www.ntslibrary.com/PDF%20Books/Wesley_Journal.pdf.

8 Wesley, 38.

CHAPTER 2

1 *Alcoholics Anonymous: The Story of How Many Thousands of Men and Women have Recovered from Alcoholism* (New York: Alcoholics Anonymous World Services, 2001), xxv.

2 *Alcoholics Anonymous*, xxv–xxxi.

3 From AA World Services, accessed August 8, 2019, https://www.aa.org/pages/en_US/aa-around-the-world.

4 "*Time* 100: The Most Important People of the Century," *Time*, 1999; Susan Cheever, "Bill W.: The Healer," *Time*, Monday, June 14, 1999, http://content.time.com/time/subscriber/article/0,33009,991266,00.html; "Time 100 Persons of the Century," *Time*, June 6, 1999, http://content.time.com/time/magazine/article/0,9171,26473,00.html.

5 Alcoholics Anonymous, *Big Book*, 4th ed. (New York: Alcoholics Anonymous World Services, 2001), foreword to the 4th edition.

6 "The Twelve Steps of AA," Alcoholics Anonymous, accessed July 8, 2021, https://aa.org.au/members/three-legacies/twelve-steps/.

7 Staff Writer, "What Is the Full Text of the Original 'Serenity Prayer' by Reinhold Niebuhr?" Reference.com, April 8, 2020, https://www.reference.com/worldview/full-text-original-serenity-prayer-reinhold-niebuhr-5661eb802a2dbacb

CHAPTER 3

1 Apostles' Creed.

CHAPTER 4

1 S. Philip Nolte and Yolanda Dreyer, "The Paradox of Being a Wounded Healer: Henri J. M. Nouwen's Contribution to Pastoral Theology," *HTS Teologiese Studies/Theological Studies* 66, no. 2 (November 1, 2010): e-4, https://doi.org/10.4102/hts.v66i2.861.

2 Nolte and Dreyer, e-2.

3 Dallas Willard, *Renovation of the Heart: Putting on the Character of Christ* (Colorado Springs: NavPress, 2012), 36.

CHAPTER 5

1 Amy Hollingsworth, *The Simple Faith of Mister Rogers: Spiritual Insights from the World's Most Beloved Neighbor* (Nashville: Integrity, 2005), 125.

2 Hollingsworth, 123.

3 Kirsten Weir, "Maximizing Children's Resilience," *American Psychological Association* 48, no. 8 (September 2017): 40, https://www.apa.org/monitor/2017/09/cover-resilience.

4 Madelieine L'Engle, *A Wind in the Door* (New York: Farrar, Straus & Giroux, 1973), 56, 99.

5 Brennan Manning, *Abba's Child: The Cry of the Heart for Intimate Belonging* (Colorado Springs, CO: NavPress, 2015), 17.

6 Manning, 16–17.

CHAPTER 6

1 Victor Hugo and Hubert Juin, *Choses vues: souvenirs, journaux, cahiers (1870–1885)* (Paris: Gallimard, 1985) 371, 521n1.

2 Victor Hugo and Pierre Seghers, *Victor Hugo, visionnaire: [illustrations et poèmes]* (Paris: R. Laffont, 1983), 10.

3 Fred Rogers, *The World According to Mr. Rogers: Important Things to Remember* (New York: Hachette, 2003), n.p.

4 Martin Luther King Jr., *Strength to Love* (Minneapolis: Fortress, 2010), 45.

5 Parker J. Palmer, *Let Your Life Speak: Listening for the Voice of Vocation* (San Francisco: Jossey-Bass, 2000), 69.

6 See Nouwen, *The Wounded Healer*, xvi (see chap. 1, n. 4).

7 Nadia Weber, *Pastrix: The Cranky, Beautiful Faith of a Sinner & Saint* (New York: Jericho Books, 2013), 50.

CHAPTER 7

1 C. S. Lewis, *The Weight of Glory* (New York: HarperOne, 1949), 26.

2 Jim Devlin, ed., *Leonard Cohen: In His Own Words* (Omnibus, 1999), 96.

3 Eddie Redmayne, Aaron Tveit and Students, "ABC Café / Red and Black" by Claude-Michel Schönberg and Herbert Kretzmer, in *Les Misérables: Highlights from the Motion Picture Soundtrack*. 2012.

CHAPTER 8

1 Phillip Randolph, master of ceremonies for the march on Washington, was the first to use this title for King, when introducing him to deliver his famous "I Have a Dream" speech.

2 Martin Luther King Jr., "Letter from a Birmingham Jail," Aptil 16, 1963, https://swap.stanford.edu/20141218230016/http://mlk-kpp01.stanford.edu/kingweb/popular_requests/frequentdocs/birmingham.pdf, 1.

3 The language of (re)signing metaphors comes from Crystal Downing, *Changing Signs of Truth: A Christian Introduction to the Semiotics of Communication* (Downers Grove, IL: IVP Academic, 2012), 305–6.

4 Martin Luther King Jr., "Loving Your Enemies," sermon, Dexter Avenue Baptist Church, Montgomery, Alabama, November 17, 1957, http://ipoet.com/ARCHIVE/BEYOND/King-Jr/Loving-Your-Enemies.html.

5 Mark Miclette, "Marion County Jail in Florida – Visiting, Searching, Contacting an Inmate," *Jail Exchange* (blog), accessed July 12, 2021, https://www.jailexchange.com/jail_and_inmate_search_blog/county-jails-by-state/marion-county-jail-in-florida-visiting-searching-contacting-an-inmate/.

6 King, "I Have a Dream" speech, August 28, 1963, https://www.foxnews.com/us/transcript-of-martin-luther-king-jr-s-i-have-a-dream-speech.

7 Martin Luther King Jr., "Where Do We Go from Here?" (speech), Atlanta, Georgia, August 16, 1967, https://kinginstitute.stanford.edu/where-do-we-go-here.

CHAPTER 9

1 Michael Beck and Rosario Picardo, *Fresh Expressions in a Digital Age: How the Church Can Prepare for a Post Pandemic World* (Nashville: Abingdon, 2021).

2 "A new life has been given us or, if you prefer, 'a design for living' that really works." Alcoholics Anonymous, *Big Book*, 28 (see chap. 2, n. 5).

3 The Layman with a Notebook, *What Is the Oxford Group?* (London: Oxford University Press, 1933), https://stepstudy.files.wordpress.com/2008/05/what_is.pdf, 6.

4 The Layman with a Notebook, 8.

5 The Layman with a Notebook, 9.

6 Alcoholics Anonymous, *Big Book*.

7 "The Twelve Steps of AA" (see chap. 2, n. 6).

CHAPTER 10

1 John Read, *Catherine Booth: Laying the Theological Foundations of a Radical Movement* (Eugene, OR: Pickwick, 2013), 6–7.

2 Read, 7

3 Read, 7.

4 Read, 8.

5 Read, 14.

6 Read, 25.

7 Malala Yousafzai, *I Am Malala: The Girl Who Stood Up for Education and Was Shot by the Taliban* (London: Weidenfeld and Nicolson,), 1–3.

8 My experience of poverty, abuse, abandonment, and incarceration has caused me to resonate deeply with the liberating God of Black Theology. See James H. Cone, *A Black Theology of Liberation* (Maryknoll, NY: Orbis, 1990), 3.

9 Matthew Clarke, "Long-Term Recidivism Studies Show High Arrest Rates," *Prison Legal News*, May 3, 2019, 60, https://www.prisonlegalnews.org/news/2019/may/3/long-term-recidivism-studies-show-high-arrest-rates/.

CHAPTER 11

1 Health Research Funding, "39 Shocking Sexual Addiction Recovery Statistics," HRF, accessed July 13, 2021, https://healthresearchfunding.org/39-shocking-sexual-addiction-recovery-statistics/.

CHAPTER 12

1 Virginie Adane, "The Penelope Stout Story: Evolution of a New Netherland Narrative," *de Halve Maen* (Fall 2009): 51–58, https://www.academia.edu/42594855/The_Penelope_Stout_Story_Evolution_of_a_New_Netherland_Narrative.

2 Leonard Sweet, *11 Indispensable Relationships You Can't Be Without* (Colorado Springs: David C. Cook, 2008), 19–20.

3 Personal conversation with Rev. Walter Edwards, July 2009, Ocala, FL.

4 Personal conversation with Dr. Len Sweet, September 6, 2017, Portland, Oregon.

CHAPTER 13

1 J. T. Owen, *Elon Musk: The Unauthorized Autobiography* (independently published, 2018), 17.

2 Edwin H. Friedman, *A Failure of Nerve: Leadership in the Age of the Quick Fix* (New York: Seabury Books, 2007), 33.

3 James Macintyre, "The Growth of UK Pioneer Missionaries for Jesus—and the Gift of Not Fitting into Social Norms," *Christian Today*, July 12, 2017, https://www.christiantoday.com/article/the.growth.of.uk.pioneer.missionaries.for.jesus.and.the.gift.of.not.fitting.into.social.norms/110671.htm.

4 Len Wilson, *Greater Things* (Plano TX: Invite Resources, 2021).

5 Woods and Wood, *Words and Witnesses*, 121–22 (see intro., n. 1).

6 Woods and Wood, 125.

7 Kevin F. Brien, *The Ignatian Adventure: Experiencing the Spiritual Exercises of Saint Ignatius in Daily Life* (Chicago: Loyola Press, 2011).

8 "Default Mode Network," *Psychology Today*, accessed July 13, 2021, https://www.psychologytoday.com/us/basics/default-mode-network.

9 MasterClass Staff, "Default Mode Network: How Meditation Affects Brain Function," MasterClass, upd. February 16, 2021, https://www.masterclass.com/articles/default-mode-network-explained#want-to-learn-even-more-about-cultivating-a-mindfulness-practice.

CHAPTER 14

1 Harry E. Eiss, *Christ of the Coal Yards: A Critical Biography of Vincent van Gogh* (Newcastle upon Tyne, UK: Cambridge Scholars, 2010), 5.

2 Eiss, 5.

3 Thomas à Kempis, *The Imitation of Christ*, trans. Aloysius Croft and Harold Bolton (Mineola, NY: Dover Publications, 2003).

4 Eiss, *Christ of the Coal Yards*, 14.

5 Eiss, 24.

6 Eiss, 24.

7 Brennan Manning with John Blase, *All Is Grace: A Ragamuffin's Memoirs* (Colorado Springs: David C. Cook, 2011), 122–23.

8 Wilson, *Greater Things* (see chap. 13, n. 4).

9 John Wesley, *The Journal of the Reverend John Wesley, A.M.: Sometime Fellow of Lincoln College, Oxford,* 2 vols. (New York: J. Emory and B. Waugh, 1832), 1:138.

10 Ken Carter, Service of Ordination address July, 2014, Lakeland, FL.

11 This is a term I first coined to describe missional and attractional forms of church living together in the same congregation. See Michael Beck, *Deep Roots, Wild Branches: Revitalizing the Church in the Blended Ecology* (Franklin, TN: Seedbed, 2019).

12 Personal conversation with Dr. Steve Harper, 2013, Orlando, FL.

13 Frederick Buechner, *Wishful Thinking: A Seeker's ABC* (New York: HarperOne, 1993), 118.

CHAPTER 15

1 Jay-Z and Kanye West, "No Church in the Wild," by Kanye West et al., in *Watch the Throne*, Roc-A-Fella Records, Roc Nation, and Def Jam Recordings, 2011, album.

2 David J. Epstein, *Range: Why Generalists Triumph in a Specialized World* (New York: Riverhead Books, 2019), 58–61.

3 Karl Heller, *Antonio Vivaldi: The Red Priest of Venice* (Portland: Amadeus, 1997), 27.

4 Makungu M. Akinyela, "Testimony of Hope: African Centered Praxis for Therapeutic Ends," *Journal of Systemic Therapies* 24.1 (2005): 5-18. https://www.academia.edu/2324704/Testimony_of_hope_African_centered_praxis_for_therapeutic_ends

5 See the Fresh Expressions website: https://freshexpressionsus.org/.

6 The Florida Conference of the United Methodist Church, "In the District," *NCD April 2021 Newsletter*, https://www.flumc.org/ncd-april-2021-newsletter.

7 A "cardinal doctrinal principle of the churches of the 16th-century Reformation, both Lutheran and Reformed, and the Protestant Free churches that arose from the Reformation churches." The Editors of Encyclopaedia Britannica,

Britannica.com, s.v. "priesthood of all believers," accessed July 14, 2021, https://www.britannica.com/topic/priesthood-of-all-believers.

8 Etsy, "Meet One of Japan's Last Remaining Sword Makers," November 15, 2011, YouTube video, 3:57, https://youtu.be/PSZKGzGqOt0.

9 National Institute on Drug Abuse, "Overdose Death Rates," NIH, January 29, 2021, https://www.drugabuse.gov/drug-topics/trends-statistics/overdose-death-rates.